Debt is double edged sword and is the economical basis of our society, you could either owe it or own it...

-Dean Anastos

Learn How to Make Money with Bank Originated Notes

Industry Secrets Revealed

Learn to Make Money with Bank-Originated Notes

"Industry Secrets Revealed"

Copyright ©2015 by Dean Anastos and Ricky Brava

All rights reserved.

Financial House Publishers

New York, NY

Disclaimer©

No part of this book can be stored, reproduced or transmitted in any form including print, recording, scanning, photocopying or electronic without prior written permission from the authors. The information presented in this book is solely for educational and entertainment purposes only. While the authors have made utmost efforts to ensure accuracy of the contents herein, the readers are advised to follow the information at their own risk. This book does not consider personal situations, so it may not be suitable for every purpose. All readers are encouraged to seek professional advice where needed. The authors and/or publisher cannot be held responsible for any personal or commercial damage that results due to misinterpretation of guidelines and ideas presented in this book. All readers are advised not to rely on the information contained in this book in making financial or investment decisions. Readers should also consult with their legal and tax advisors before making any investment. This book cannot be used as a substitute for professional advice. This book is for educational and entertainment purposes only. This book is merely our opinions, our thoughts and our conclusions. Again, it is for educational and entertainment purposes only, and you -- and only you -- are responsible if you choose to do anything based on what you read.

What You'll Find In This Book

Making money can be very simple, but you have to do it the right way. When you talk about making money, most people see it as a discussion on complex mathematics and volatile economic conditions. However, things are not so complicated. If you are really excited to take immediate steps and start making money with a little help from bank notes, you've come to the right place. This book will give you a comprehensive review of how notes can help you make more money. You'll also find useful information about other money-making options. In addition, this book gives tips and real life experiences pertaining to how you can make the most of notes and claim a real financial win. You are about to read a simple, entertaining and effective plan to make numbers work your way. Let's get started, and explore money-making ideas and notes in more detail.

Who is this information for

Entrepreneurs, business owners, self-starters, real estate investors, financiers, the socially conscious, visionaries -- people who want to design a life, not just make a living – this is for you.

This book is a collaboration between two self-made men who are truly doing the work in today's market -- and are very successful at it. Along the way, we have started some of the "gurus" in this industry on their way to success. We have created winners and millionaires and, in the meantime, changed the American economic situation one note at a time.

If you are someone who wants more clarity on the note business... If you are seeking answers, and you are smart enough not simply to follow any educator for no good reason other than that you saw him/her at a conference... Then this book is for you.

We wrote this book for you to have access to our note experiences and know-how without having to pay for a mentor, a workshop, or get on any figurative ride. This way, you will have the information you need to succeed in this business and to be *at the top of the food chain*, as we like to call it.

Table of Contents

WHAT YOU'LL FIND IN THIS BOOK   8

WHO IS THIS INFORMATION FOR   9

TABLE OF CONTENTS   11

CHAPTER ONE   15

THE SECRET TO MAKING BIG MONEY

CHAPTER TWO   27

INVESTING IN REAL ESTATE: WHAT ARE YOUR OPTIONS

CHAPTER THREE   37

BANK NOTES VS.

SELLER-FINANCED NOTES

CHAPTER FOUR 45

GETTING STARTED WITH

NON-PERFORMING BANK NOTES

CHAPTER FIVE 55

SECRETS TO ACQUIRING

THE BEST NOTES

CHAPTER SIX 65

DO'S AND DON'TS OF PURCHASING

CHAPTER SEVEN 73

SERVICING THE NOTES

– WHAT YOU NEED TO KNOW

CHAPTER EIGHT 79

WANT TO EXIT:

LEARN HOW YOU CAN USE POPULAR EXIT STRATEGIES

CHAPTER NINE 85

PET PEEVES

AFTERWORD 87

GLOSSARY 91

ACKNOWLEDGMENTS 191

ABOUT THE AUTHORS 195

Chapter One

The Secret to Making Big Money

Should you listen to what money has to say? You don't have to be a financial expert to understand how important money is and what you can do with it. We live in a world that is sophisticated and complicated to a certain degree. Interestingly, every person you meet has a different answer to how money can change your life. Money sometimes is also blamed to be the proverbial root of all evil, but *making* money is not always an evil deed. It's up to you to decide how you will see the world after you become wealthy. If you still doubt the importance of money, it is time you take a close look at the financial conditions and economic systems prevalent in the world today.

The financial system is closely related to every single industry. It is safe to say that if you don't have money, it is not easy to survive. Having said this, you can also guarantee a better life by making more money.

Sounds good, right? This is also good news for those who are still trying to recover from the effects of the recession.

One of the most obvious advantages of making money is that it saves you on the rainiest days. Nobody knows what tomorrow will bring. Things can fall apart quite quickly, and having money to spare can be your greatest protection.

Your Top Money-Making Options

Contrary to what you see and hear about the market conditions, you do have good chances of making money. By the time you reach the end of this book, you will see that the amount of wealth you build depends on the decisions you make.

Your Own Business

Starting your own business is by far the best opportunity. Many people would also tell you that this is your ideal chance to invest in gold and other precious metals to make quick cash. Buying real estate is also a huge money-making option. Don't forget to check out the next chapter to know more about opportunities offered by real estate.

The Internet as a Vehicle for Profit

When it comes to money making ideas, you can never ignore the power of the Internet. Yet another option to make money is through online and affiliate marketing. Both have created a lot of hype, and you can now make money sitting comfortably at home. You can also reach a worldwide audience 24/7 -- something that is nearly impossible with traditional marketing tactics.

Because the Internet connects you with a large number of people instantly, you can also use it to attract new employers. You can make money by getting a new job, plus enjoy doing your work.

There are numerous other ways you can earn your fortune. For instance, you could settle for making money on popular websites such as eBay. In fact, over approximately 2 million people earn extra cash by selling on online auction websites such as eBay and Amazon. There's no reason why you shouldn't try. It only takes a little bit of practice to master selling and start making cash online. Your benefits just don't end here. You have flexible working hours and you are your own boss.

Low starting costs mean that you can make higher profits when running your own business. Corporate giants accomplish great feats, but they also have large costs to handle. Your online or home-based business has lower costs, so when compared to corporate giants, you can easily afford to specialize your products and services to meet the demands of your customers.

You can use the Internet to make the biggest difference in the size of your audience. Even a small home-based business can yield huge returns if you spread the word the right way. Make sure you keep your website updated so that your customers and interested parties keep coming back to know more.

If you have dreamt about making lots of cash by starting your own business, the internet gives you a chance to actually try doing it. You don't need to make a large investment. If running a full-fledged online business feels like a daunting task, you can make money with a more manageable option: selling things that you no longer want or need.

Dig out items you never use. This can include items like music equipment, CDs, clothes, toys and anything that does not deserve a place in your home. Put an attractive advertisement on a local classified website such as www.CraigsList.org. You likely will be able to sell your unused items within a couple of hours if you price them reasonably. As mentioned earlier, you can even auction your items on websites such as Amazon and eBay.

For many reasons, Amazon and Craigslist have what it takes to attract large audiences, and you can actually find a great deal of prospective customers. In other words, you can use them as a platform to sell your "junk." *Remember, what you consider junk can be a valuable treasure for any other person.*

Since the most difficult part of any business is attracting a large number of sales, make sure your ads are unique and attractive enough to hook your customer. Many people flock to Amazon and eBay to sell their wares, so it is important you stand out in the crowd.

Franchises

You also have the opportunity to earn lots of cash by joining the corporate giants. Not sure what this means? The strongest option in this context is to own a franchise. Even the most established businesses can come to you if you have the right location. All you need to do is own a franchise first. The bottom line is that owning a franchise can be one of the easiest ways to achieve true financial freedom.

It's tough to make a statement about which franchise is going to work, but it is best to go for a deal that makes sense to you. You surely know what your interests are and where you want to see yourself after a few years. Use this information to help you in making your decision.

As mentioned earlier, your financial success -- more than anything else -- depends on your own decisions. If you choose the franchise route, for instance, go for it, and treat it as your own business. The smarter and harder you work, the greater the rewards.

Investment Vehicles

If you are still not impressed by these money-making options, there are other ways to maximize your cash reserves. Try investing in stocks, and – if done properly and with some luck – you can make the most of your money. Remember, stock investments -- when made intelligently -- not only protect the money you have put in the market, but also likely will yield a good return on investment. Like every other business, you have to do your homework before deciding to invest in a company's stock.

The primary reason you put your money in stocks is to reap valuable rewards. Even though stock markets seem scary, rest assured that they are not. Buying a stock means that you are buying part of a company. Technically, you "invest" money in companies that are making profits.

Keep in mind that stock investment proves to be particularly useful when there is a bullish trend in the market. So before you invest your money, it is better if you have a clear idea about why you are investing in the stock of a particular company.

You can continue to monitor the stock market and take appropriate decisions to put extra cash in your hands. In order to make the most of your investment, you can spread your money in a number of different stocks, diversifying your portfolio.

You surely want to make money as quickly as possible, and there's nothing wrong with that. Financial experts suggest that buying CD's (Certificate of Deposit) and bonds is also a good way to make your investments more secure. You don't need to have an MBA degree to beef up your bank accounts.

The key to successful investing (making more money) is not trying to do anything special. If you want to make great returns, the process is not that complicated.

Holding a few bonds together with stocks is not a bad thing to do. In addition to the initial cost, the only thing that matters the most is having variety in your investment portfolio. You can even boost your returns and profits by finding the right combination.

You can hold stocks when you have a long time to invest and then gradually shift to bonds. Not many people are keen to invest in stocks at this point -- especially after the events of the recession.

Remember, the trick to make profits here is keeping your eyes on your long-term goals. It may take a little time for the stock market to recover, but you need to keep your various investments on track.

If investing directly in the stock market seems too risky for you, according to a few experts, investing in mutual funds is a much safer option. Again, the stock market does have greater risk; however, you cannot ignore the fact that people have made millions after investing in it.

There is no harm in being a little careful when you invest money. You can have a variety of stocks, bonds, mutual funds and CDs in your portfolio to make a little more money on your investment. The only thing you really need to do to become successful is to understand how different investments really work.

Financial experts also believe that buying gold and other precious metals at this point in time is another good investment. There is no commodity that can match the "gold" standard. So, if you own a little piece of this precious metal now, you could you make lots of money later. Gold, for ages now, is an indicator of wealth and holds much higher value than currency notes.

Money can make some of the most remarkable things happen very quickly. Your home can become larger and your old vehicle can be traded in for the most luxurious car. Life can get good when you are willing to make an effort and you do have a lot of options to make and save money.

Unfortunately, there is no shortcut to earning a few extra bucks. If you really want to sustain the numbers that are rolling in, get creative and capitalize on every opportunity that is coming your way. You might have heard exciting stories about people making tons of cash in real estate. This definitely has made some of you curious to know more about the potential of real estate -- and the next chapter of this book will give you more information on just that. Don't forget to check out the next section to get familiar with the ways you can make cash by investing in real estate.

Chapter Two

Investing in Real Estate: What are Your Options

People believe that there is one simple secret to successful investing and that is through real estate. Don't be surprised when your friends encourage you to buy a property and wait for its value to increase.

Normally, buying homes at lower prices and then selling them at shooting prices is what is considered the hottest trend in real estate. Experts predict that these older ways of real estate investing are going to change. This is mainly because customers have become more informed and perhaps smarter than what they used to be.

Having said all this, making money in real estate is not rocket science. The fact is that you can make extra cash by knowing the three basic principles of this business:

1. You have to buy a product or service at the best price;
2. You have to sell the same at a price higher than what you purchased it; and
3. You have to achieve all this in a measurable period of time.

These principles shouldn't be difficult to understand. Technically, the real estate business is all about selling your -product at a higher price than what you had paid to buy it.

Buying property at the best price means that you need to purchase land or any other property at a price lower than the trending market value. Mastering this is both a science and an art, but don't let that intimidate you if you're a novice. There are techniques that can help you achieve this with great ease.

When it comes to money-making options in real estate, there are a few proven ways to do it. Real estate investors earn rewards by:

1. The increase in value of property they've purchased;
2. Leasing out their property to tenants and other customers; and
3. Making profits on business that depends on real estate.

Interestingly, regardless of what real estate pundits predict, the basic ways of making money in real estate have not changed much.

Appreciation or Increase in Value

The most common and perhaps, the most basic way of earning extra bucks in real estate is the increase of value of the property in question. Make sure you keep a close eye on the increasing market prices so that you can make thousands of dollars in return for your deal. You may even consider renovations to beautify and increase the property value.

Investment in Undeveloped Land

This is something that seems to stay in demand regardless of the existing dollar value or other real estate trends. Cities continue to expand and, as a result, the undeveloped land on its periphery becomes more valuable. Developers are very keen to buy undeveloped land and this increases your chances of making huge profits.

When investing in undeveloped land, there also exists the possibility of discovery of valuable minerals and other rare earth metals. You will definitely become a millionaire if you discover oil reserves, but mineral deposits can also make you rich.

Investment in Residential Property

There are a number of lucrative deals for you to make money in real estate in the form of foreclosed homes. Just because the home was foreclosed on, doesn't mean it cannot resell. You can invest in foreclosed homes, and help it find a new owner.

You must, however keep a few things in mind. If you are planning to buy a foreclosed home as an investment, do not go for a home that needs major work.

Become a detective, and do inspect the homes before you buy them. You can also talk to neighbors to know more about the previous owners, the house and the property. If you find that the home requires a costly makeover, you should continue your search.

You can generate a generous stream of cash with the help of real estate investment *only* when you assess the property carefully before you buy it. Remember, real estate investment is not an ordinary occurrence. The fate of your investment is determined largely at the very moment you make a purchase.

When looking at residential properties, location and neighborhood are the biggest factors you have to consider. The best homes in an evolving neighborhood are always in great demand and small home improvements can increase the price. This is one of the common techniques used by property flippers to increase their profits.

Making Money by Leasing Residential and Commercial Properties

Buying property is not the only way of making money in real estate. If you own an apartment or an office building, you can charge other people for using your property. The good news is that you can lease both residential and commercial properties. Here are some simple tricks to help you make more money by leasing your real estate property.

1. First, figure out the total income you expect after leasing your property.
2. Estimate the total expenses involved in leasing your property. The amount you charge your tenant should cover your mortgage payment, taxes, and all other costs.
3. Make sure you lease property in an area that has high listings. You will be able to attract more tenants in areas where there is unusually high demand for the rental property.

Investment in Short Sales And REO Property

Short sales and investment in REO property are two major areas that are still ignored by real estate investors. Most investors do not think twice before buying homes after a short sale. While you have to be careful when signing a deal, investing in short sales and REO properties is definitely not a bad move.

Typically, the term *short sale* is used when a real estate property is going through a foreclosure. Since the property is in default (the owner did not pay the mortgage), the lenders are looking for the next best option in terms of selling. This is your chance to purchase the property for a price lower than the original amount owed on it.

A real estate property is said to be an REO property when foreclosure is legally completed. The home or piece of land is now owned by the mortgage lender. On most occasions, the lender is a bank or any other financial institution. REO stands for "Real Estate

Owned. Real estate investments usually become a lot easier when you seek professional help from a broker or a real estate agent. Working together with someone who has the right qualifications can help familiarize you with the twists and turns of this business. Having good support during investment in short sales and REO properties increases your chances of making long-term profits.

Another factor to take into consideration is the number of foreclosures in the market. The higher the number is, the more options you have when it comes to REO properties. Banks and other financial institutions want to get rid of the large number of vacant homes and office buildings they have acquired. You can use this opportunity to buy property below the current market value. The lower the price you pay, the higher your chances are of making profits.

So if you are seriously looking to make cash, don't forget to include short sales and REO properties on your list of dream properties. This rule can be applied to any potential property, and make sure you do your homework before making a final decision.

Now that you have a good idea of the real estate options that are available to you for reaping high profits, we will move on to the next chapter that will shed light on the two most significant types of notes for money making real estate investments, bank notes and seller-financed notes. The next section will also explain where bank notes score and how they can help you secure your desired financial gains.

Chapter Three

Bank Notes vs. Seller-Financed Notes

Buyers are edgy, lenders are tight-fisted, and appraisers are becoming increasingly picky. Whether you intend to purchase a house or sell one, the competition is downright aggressive when it comes to real estate investments. However, with the availability of financing options like seller-financed notes and bank notes, a real estate investment is now a dream come true for a vast majority of individuals.

Given the recent tumultuous economic times, anyone considering a real estate investment will want to evaluate all the benefits and opportunities that exist before taking the proverbial leap. Bank notes and seller-financed notes are financing options that can help an investor grow. Before delving into the details as to what will work wonders for you, it is imperative to understand what these two financing options actually are and how they fit into the big picture.

What Are Bank Notes?

Bank notes are, in essence, conventional financing. The lending institution (the bank) lends the desired amount of money to the buyer so that s/he can pay off the purchase price of the property. The bank, in turn, takes a security interest for the property. Here, it is important to understand that this security interest comes as a deed of trust or mortgage. Using this deed of trust, the bank secures the right to foreclose the property to reimburse the loan amount in case of default.

In the case of bank notes, the buyer pays the seller using the amount borrowed from the bank, and the seller no longer has any role in the scenario. With the seller now out of the picture, the buyer is responsible for making timely payments to the bank until the loan is completely paid off, and the buyer can claim the possession of the property.

What Are Seller-Financed Notes?

Unlike bank notes, seller-financed notes keep the seller bound to the buyer in a financial relationship until the property's price is paid off. What happens in the seller-financed note scenario is that the seller does not get a lump sum amount of money. Instead, the title of the house's ownership is transferred to the seller, and the buyer assumes the role of the lender for the security interest and note. This note is paid off in a manner akin to a mortgage. It is the seller, however, that receives it -- not the bank. In addition, just like traditional financing, the seller has the power to foreclose a property in case default is detected.

In other words, one can say that a seller-financed note is a kind of transaction where the seller offers the loan to a buyer instead of a bank. There are no prerequisites to a seller-financed note, and both the seller's and buyer's interests are protected using a legally binding document.

Why Choose Bank Notes Instead of Seller-Financed Notes?

While seller-financed notes may come as a convenience to all those who feel that they can be real estate investors despite having a colorful credit history, what cannot be ignored is that things are not always as they seem. Seller-financed notes do have several downsides associated with them -- many of which most investors are unaware. While there are several reasons as to why you should prefer bank notes over seller financed notes, a handful of the most notable ones are briefly listed below.

Bank Notes Are Common

As a seller, you won't appreciate the arrangement that seller-financed notes imply. A seller may typically have objections such as not having enough money to lend to a buyer and not being inclined towards becoming a lender considering the risks involved. Also, in most of the cases, a seller needs complete proceeds from her/his last sale to purchase the next property. For such real estate investors, seller-financed notes are not even an option.

In contrast to seller-financed notes, bank notes are common, and there is a constant supply of these notes. As a result, an investor can secure them at any time of the year. Unlike seller-financed notes which are hard to come by, bank notes are easily available -- and this is definitely where bank notes score.

Bank Notes Are Hassle-Free

Regardless of the kind of investment, every investor wants the whole process to be as effortless as possible. Sadly, in the case of seller-financed notes, this is something that simply does not happen. The chances of finding seller-financed notes are very rare in the first place. If you do find them, it is the result of combing through county records – a potentially time-consuming process which is something most investors find exceedingly frustrating.

While one may believe that since no lending institution is involved in the seller financed notes scenario, there will be less paperwork involved. The truth is that obtaining a bank note is far easier compared to obtaining a seller-financed note, by all means.

It Is Cheaper to Reach Out to Note Holders

It is obvious that while In the case of bank notes, the case of bank notes, the interested parties go to the bank themselves, while in the case of seller-financed notes, the seller has to make efforts to reach out to those who might be interested. For instance, mass mail marketing is mostly used to reach potential clientele. However, a three-page sales letter highlighting the property's pluses is not often worth the time and effort you invest into it.

On the other end of the spectrum are bank notes. They are sent out regularly, as they are originated by the banks themselves. Banks also tend to cooperate with those seeking these notes as they view it as an attempt to write off their inventory.

Leverage on Relationship of Companies with Banks

Investors consider seller-financed notes an option, believing that it takes a considerably large amount of capital to buy notes from a bank. Since they do not have that much money sitting in their accounts, they believe that resorting to seller-financed notes is the only way to do it right. All the hassles and effort it takes to get to the right person to secure bank notes are reasons enough to discourage any investor. What these investors do not know, however, is that there are certain reputable companies that have partnered with banks. This can help them smooth out all the wrinkles in the bank note game with little to no effort.

There are credible names in the business such as Mortgage Float and Apollo Financial Group. Not only do they have the network to get you through the process, but they also have the capital to help facilitate the bank note acquiring process for you.

Taking convenience a step ahead, Mortgage Float and Apollo Financial Group-- unlike their counterparts -- offer a wide array of bank notes from their pocket, among which you are bound to find one to meet your specifications. With their years of experience in the industry, companies like Mortgage Float can help you steer clear of any issues in the process of acquiring bank notes.

Having discussed the drawbacks of seller-financed notes, the next chapter will provide information as to how you can get started and how non-performing bank notes can help you remedy your ailing bank accounts.

Chapter Four

Getting Started with Non-Performing Bank Notes

Trading non-performing notes from a bank can prove to be a very profitable activity. Also, buying non-performing notes is considered to be one of the hottest trends today. Despite that, investing in bank notes is a challenge for those new to it. It is a whole new genre of real estate investing-- with the perks it has to offer rendering it a remarkable opportunity to make money.

In some respects, investing in bank notes is more fruitful than traditional real estate investing with lesser work involved, giving it an edge above all other types of real estate investing.

Investing in non-performing notes has come a long way in the last few years. Previously, one had to spend hours going through paper records, but everything now has moved online. With a few clicks, you can release the entire request without ever having to leave the confines of your home. This has not only made the process convenient for savvy investors, but also has triggered a steep rise in the number of those who are now investing in bank notes.

Before we dive into how non-performing bank notes can be valuable to any investor and how to go about obtaining them, let's take a look at what non-performing bank notes are.

What Are Non-Performing Bank Notes?

As the name implies, these are essentially loans that are generated by the banks. When a real estate property is purchased with a mortgage, this is called a note. They are not performing on the terms they were written as, and so they do not produce a cash flow.

In the event of a default (such as when the buyer misses a payment), the note becomes a non-performing bank note. In this scenario, the bank has to go through the standard procedure of the collection process and foreclosing a property. Since this procedure is costly, banks try to avoid it.

Two terminologies that you need to know when acquiring a non-performing bank note are *first lien mortgage notes* and *second lien mortgage notes.* They are briefly defined below.

First Lien Mortgage Notes

A first lien mortgage note is essentially a type of mortgage loan with interest on the note. With this, the first priority is payment -- in case the borrower defaults. First lien loans will be secured with the real estate property which serves as collateral for the loan amount.

Second Lien Mortgage Notes

Second lien mortgage notes are also backed by property. It is imperative to understand that the property that will be pledged as collateral for this note can be the same or even overlap the property that served as collateral for the first lien loan. Also, second lien mortgage notes have a priority lower to that of first lien notes since first lien mortgage notes will be paid off first in the repayment schedule.

Now, one might wonder why a buyer would want to purchase a second lien mortgage note. Well, the answer is quite simple. Since they are riskier compared to first lien mortgage notes, they can be acquired at a much lower cost. In this scenario, the note buyer has leverage because s/he can secure the loans at larger discounts. It is key to make sure that the initial investment is comprehensively covered by the property's equity, as this will give more flexibility in case you choose to foreclose a property to recover your investment.

Why Buy Non-Performing Bank Notes?

The next question to ask is why a note buyer should purchase non-performing notes from a bank. There are several advantages to doing so, briefly explained below.

- You do not need to go through any tedious courthouse steps.
- You do not need to put time and effort into formulating marketing campaigns that are crucial to finding appropriate seller-financed notes (also known as "owner-financed notes").
- Given the declined state of the economy, defaulted notes are in abundance. Because of the constant supply of opportunities this ensures, you have many options.
- Non-performing bank notes can be acquired for a much more reasonable price. It can be perceived as blessing in disguise because you can easily start off with investment without breaking your bank. Since all the bad news is already priced in, these notes can be acquired at competitive prices.
- We all wish to have that four-hour work week business model which is next to impossible

given the recent economic meltdown. However, by trading non-performing bank notes, your dream of having a four-hour work week business model can find its realization. Investment in non-performing bank notes can be viewed as a virtual business. While it won't take as much time and effort as any mainstream business will, the profits are just as good.

- With non-performing bank notes, you are the key player. The lesser the investor is involved, the easier the management is and the higher your chances are of organizing things the way you want them. You won't have to deal with unthankful tenants that are always willing to annoy you with issues as mundane as clogged toilets.
- By trading in a non-performing bank note, you are your own boss and work at your own will. You won't have to beg banks to accept your short sale. You won't have to knock on door

after door only to have them slammed in your face. With non-performing bank notes, opportunities will come to you.
- The non-performing bank note will empower you to decide whether a short sale will go through or not.
- Since you will be the owner of the non-performing note, you have the leverage against the borrower. You will have the upper hand because the borrower will have a reason to work with you. Either they choose to work with you, or they lose their property. In any case, it is a win-win situation for you.
- What further comes as a perk is that in the event of a short sale, you essentially are the bank, and it is therefore you who decides whether it should be approved or not.
- Last but not the least, the multiple exit strategies are the cherry on top. In the case of non-performing bank notes, there are more exit strategies than deemed imaginable for any

traditional real estate investments. What further sweetens the deal is that the closing costs -- a matter of great concern for lien holders -- are not only fixed, but minimal as well.

Who Are Note Sellers?

The next thing to come to your mind must be who these note sellers are and where you can find them. For the most part, note-sellers are none other than the banks themselves. There are also companies that buy notes from the bank, and sell them to note buyers.

If you are wondering why you should buy from companies in the presence of banks, the answer is quite simple. Instead of having to deal with each real estate property individually, banks prefer to sell large portfolios that cost millions. Since it is not possible to have that much capital, you can seek out companies – like those described in the last chapter -- to acquire non-performing bank notes without breaking a sweat.

In this chapter, we understood the nitty-gritty of non-performing bank notes, what the advantages of securing them are and where those seeking such notes should start looking for them. In the next chapter, we will be revealing secrets about how to acquire notes in order to secure the best deals.

Chapter Five

Secrets to Acquiring the Best Notes

With the advantages of bank-note investing registered in your mind, the next step two-fold: First, determine how to go about the process of acquiring the best notes, and secondly, evaluate which notes will turn out to be financially beneficial options in the long run. Keep reading to arm yourself with the basics of buying a bank note before you enter the bank note market.

What you must keep in mind before getting started with the investment is as follows:

1- Cash or access to cash;

2- List of notes for sale;

3- Research tools;

4- Acquiring the note;

5- Servicing the note; and

6- Exit strategies.

Below is an explanation of each of the bullets listed above.

1- Cash or Access to Cash

""It takes money to make money," as the saying goes. You cannot make more money unless you have enough to invest. If you belong to the group of those who have summed up enough capital, you can simply go ahead, and take a dive. If all you have, however, are some savings for your rainy days, you can generate the desired substantial gains by accessing capital through your family, friends, or any partnerships you can form on reasonable terms.

As in any investment, one is often left wondering how much money is needed to get started. Frankly speaking, the amount of capital you need is highly subjective and is dependent on the type of property in which you plan to invest, in addition to the type of assets you believe will work wonders for you. Also, the amount of money you will need to invest depends on the note position you believe will help you accomplish your financial objectives.

2- List of Notes for Sale

Moving ahead, the next thing you will need is a list of notes for sale. This list is usually found in the form of a spreadsheet and is your first step in spotting a great deal.

For someone new to bank notes investment, it can be fairly overwhelming the first time you come across the list of notes for sale. It can come in handy to know the fields that you need to thoroughly check. They include property address; note payoff or the principal balance (unpaid) on the property; the position of note being offered; and the estimated market value of the property.

The above listed factors are those that you need to take into account in order to make a well-informed decision. *These factors are essential to success; therefore, each and every single opportunity should be eyed objectively.* The acquisition process itself is quite straightforward. It is the evaluation of opportunities that takes time and effort but at the end of the day, the profits that may pour in are well worth it.

3- Research Tools

The due diligence phase starts next. For the first-timer, decisions such as which notes should be purchased and how much should be offered for them can seem like an overwhelming endeavor. However, in answers to these questions, you will find your key to success as an investor.

Although there are no hard and fast rules to the due diligence phase, by doing things right at this stage, you can be well on your way to success and riches.

Once you are done with the process of identifying notes that easily fit into your budget, next you can run the information you have collected through a variety of websites. *It is imperative to understand that the due diligence phase is critical to your success, and its importance cannot be emphasized enough.* After all, it is at this stage that you can strike gold.

There are a number of websites that you can use to find answers to questions like, "What is an estimated fair price of the property?" and, "In what kind of neighborhood is it?" Some websites to help provide you with precious insight on neighborhood trends and property value are www.zillow.com and www.trulia.com. What further comes as a surprise is that these websites provide service free of cost. While you shouldn't use the result as the sole basis for your decisions, they do help you achieve a fairly good general idea of the entire scenario.

Other websites like www.zipwho.com allow you to easily grasp neighborhood demographics. Essentially this website provides information regarding the income level of an area. Using this information, you can find out if your target market resides there or not.

Other websites that can serve as valuable research tools are www.realquest.com, www.titlesearch.com and www.localrealtors.com. The information rendered by these websites can take you a step closer to your goal of making money using bank notes.

Once you have researched to this level, the next step is contacting the note-seller and inquiring if the note you have researched is available or not. If the note-seller responds in the affirmative, you can order a BPO (Broker Price Opinion) right away. A BPO is, as the name implies, the value of a property estimated by a real estate broker, a firm or any individual qualified to do so. The BPO solely depends on the characteristics of the property under consideration.

Now that we live in a world where most everything has gone online, you need not skim through yellow pages to find competent brokers. There are websites that have networked with the best brokers in the business to help you accomplish this feat.

For instance, www.summitvaluations.com is a company offering BPOs for as low as $100. Usually, you receive a response within three business days. While you are waiting for the BPO, you should not just sit around and wait. In the meantime, you can check the county title records to verify that the lien and lien position you have found are correct.

Some sources you can use are www.protitleusa.com and www.realquest.com. They can check the title for you for a fee ranging from $100 to $200. One important thing to keep in mind is to search for liens and any outstanding property taxes that exist against the property. The liens that you should take into account are water liens and property tax liens. Both of these types of liens are super liens relative to first mortgage.

In this scenario, typically, a communication gap exists between the buyer and the seller, as the seller believes that a property is worth more, and the buyer is of the opinion that the price is simply too high. What both parties cannot overlook are the other costs that are involved such as the ones previously mentioned. This also leads to a number of issues when it comes to foreclosures. Other liens such as IRS liens, judgment liens and mechanic liens are not a big hassle as they are subordinate liens that can easily be wiped out in foreclosure.

4- Acquiring the Note

One of the most crucial steps of the entire process is acquiring the bank note. Once you have accepted an offer, you will receive a Purchase Sale Agreement (PSA). A PSA is a legally binding contract that obligates a buyer to make a purchase and the seller to sell a particular product or service. It is used to protect or finalize the interest of both the parties before they agree to close a deal.

Next, you have to transfer the funds to the note seller. To transfer the funds in this business means to wire the funds in one or two business days. Within 30-40 days, you will receive your assignment and collateral package. An assignment is used to assign the ownership of the deed of trust or mortgage to the new party. In other words, one can say that it is at this stage that the note-holder transfers all the rights to the note-buyer. A collateral package, on the other hand, is comprised of the original signed note and mortgage.

There are certain steps that are strongly recommended you take at this stage. These steps will ensure that you do not have to deal with any unwelcomed inconveniences in the future. These steps are listed below.

- First and foremost, make sure you record your assignment with the county.
- Further correspondence will be needed with the county to find answers to questions like

where the assignment should be mailed. You will be informed about the charges that you will incur (these charges can range anywhere from $5 to $60, as they vary from one county to another).

The next chapter will elaborate, in detail, the do's and don'ts of purchasing non-performing bank notes.

Chapter Six

Do's and Don'ts of Purchasing Non-Performing Bank Notes

Before we move on to the section about note servicing, let's take a look at do's and don'ts of purchasing bank notes.

If you are planning to buy a non-performing bank note, keep in mind that the financial institution or bank currently holding it does not want it. Banks are meant to lend money to generate profits. They are not in business to manage disposition of real estate properties, let alone juggle between property taxes that are long overdue, not to mention the infuriating insurance premiums and maintenance costs that non-performing bank notes incur.

When the property reverts back to the bank, in the event of a default on the home loan, the holding costs of the foreclosed property start mounting. That is why most of the lenders are eager to get rid of any non-performing assets as soon as possible -- often at substantial discounts.

The main concern of the bank is to recover some of the capital tied up in this mortgage. They strive to accomplish it by hunting for low-maintenance loan situations. When it comes to questions like what a buyer will derive out of such an arrangement, the answer is: a clean title of the property with all encumbrances and liens-related issues appropriately resolved.

A tip for all those planning to invest in non-performing bank notes is to do comparison shopping. It is strongly recommended that you take the time to shop around because there are several institutions you will come across that are willing to offer these loans at reasonable terms.

When you come across one such loan, remember that the bank or lending institution has expertise of handling real estate. They can easily negotiate a good deal with a focus on your individual needs, but if they do not take into account your needs, you can always walk away. There are other fish in the sea, and you likely will never run out of options.

When it comes to a non-performing bank note, a well-informed decision cannot be stressed enough. Investment in non-performing bank notes can create not only passive income for you but cash flow as well – depending on the outcome you desire.

It can be your chance of improving things for yourself on the financial front. By taking advantage of the deep discounts that are offered, the investor can access real estate property upon foreclosure without any hassles.

This implies that you no longer will have to deal with any frustrating landlord/tenant issues. You are saved of all the annoyances because, in this scenario, you are the boss. It is *you* who controls the process, and it is *you* who acts as the bank.

If any downsides of investing in non-performing bank notes are to be stated, the only one is competition. Non-performing bank notes mean a real estate property with a clean title at unbelievable discounts. Who wouldn't want to snag a deal like this? However, the story does not end here. You can achieve that competitive advantage by establishing friendly relationships with your lender.

Also, you can have that edge above others by touting your credit report to your potential lender This will help them realize that you are someone they can trust. Imagine their distress when they find out that a property they have recently disposed of landed back in their lap just because of the same old bad credit story with someone else.

As touched upon before, one can find these non-performing bank notes with large and small lenders and banks. You can start by contacting regional or local banks in your area. Meeting their portfolio management or asset management team is helpful in building that relationship and trust. There are countless listing sites as well as web-based databases where you can find such non-performing bank notes for sale. Now, let's take a look at some do's and don'ts that you should keep in mind before purchasing a non-performing bank note.

DO's

- ***DO review the BPO for every single real estate property.*** It is of grave importance as the BPO supplements the review of loan files. In addition, you should also take time to evaluate factors such as collection commentaries; asset inspections; title research; servicing records; tax information, to name a few.
- ***DO make sure that you have the capital necessary in place.*** Once a purchase offer is accepted, you will be expected to hand over the money right away. With so many

prospects for the same note, you may have to pay for any delay -- by entirely losing the deal.

- **DO make sure you have all the systems and internal processes in place to seamlessly transfer any assets from the sellers.**
- **DO make sure that the note servicer you choose is licensed.**

DON'Ts

- **DON'T begin by investing in multiple notes at one time.** It will likely be some time before you will get hold of things so make sure that you purchase just one or two non-performing bank notes at first.
- **DON'T pretend.** Be who you are. Misrepresenting yourself won't get you anywhere. Only humility and honesty can help keep things right on track for you.
- **DON'T look for any shortcuts when it comes to the due diligence process.** The last thing

you will want is an asset you failed to keep simply because you were in a rush to sign off the deal. We can't say this enough: At the end of the day you -- and only you -- are responsible for your own due diligence.

By employing and keeping all the factors listed above in mind, you will have no difficulty spotting an ideal non-performing bank note that will lead you to substantial gains in the long run. In the next section, we will understand the procedure of servicing a bank note you have acquired in the event need arises.

Chapter Seven

Servicing the Notes – What You Need to Know

This chapter will give a detailed explanation of note servicing, defining what it is, in addition to discussing the benefits buyers and sellers can secure through this process.

What Is Note Servicing?

As explained before, in the case of seller-financed notes, when a buyer purchases a real estate property, the seller finances the deal instead of some lending institution or bank. This deal is secured by a promissory note or real estate contract and a deed of trust. With this legally binding document in place, the buyer is obliged to make payments to the buyer according to the terms and conditions listed in the agreement.

The note-servicing phase comes once the buyer has claimed the ownership of the note. But what exactly *is* note servicing? It is quite simply the process through which payment is (1) collected from the buyer, (2) processed and (3) disbursed to the seller as per her/his instructions.

At this point, as a buyer, there are two routes you can take. You can either service the note yourself, or you can hire a third-party servicer to take care of this. A third-party servicer, however, should be preferred, as it establishes several benefits not only for the buyer but for the seller as well. These benefits are briefly delineated out below.

Benefits to the Buyer

- It establishes credit history.

- The buyer can make use of the automatic payment option.
- Annual reports of detailed account information can be pulled.
- The buyer is saved all the inconvenience of maintaining balance calculation time and again. Since amortization is accurate, it helps eliminate any disputes that may arise.
- The buyer receives assistance in title clearance because of escrow, once the entire amount is paid off.

Benefits to the Seller

While one may believe that the benefits of using third-party note services are limited to buyers only, this is not the case. It is a win-win situation for the sellers as well, since they enjoy the following advantages:

- With third-party servicers, sellers can have the IRS' reporting of interest -- often provided free of charge. This comes as a big advantage, as it

eliminates the need to provide buyers with the Social Security number which most sellers are reluctant to give.
- In most cases, sellers can use the auto-deposit option.
- Often, remarkable features such as coupons and automatic payment are provided, resulting in a timely payment history.
- Additional protection is established through optional accounts reserved for tax and insurance.

Third-party note servicers often issue free late charge notices which translates into ease for the collection of delinquent or bad debt.

Even our companies -- Apollo Financial Group and Mortgage Float -- use third party note servicers because we believe it is not just cost effective, but also because the buyer does not need to be preoccupied with the legalities involved (such as licensing). Furthermore, these servicing companies are responsible for tax forms and bookkeeping which are required by IRS – a factor that cannot be overlooked.

When it comes to note-servicing companies, one is spoiled with the amount of choices.

Note Servicing Process

The note-servicing process is quite simple. There are only three steps:

1. In the first step, investors or sellers provide notes that are to be serviced.
2. In step 2, buyers make payments and a two-way correspondence between the concerned parties is established. Often forms such as 1098 and customer service are provided as a part of the services offered.
3. In step 3, the hired note servicing company streamlines cash flow and management reports are submitted to the seller.

As this chapter ends, we have learned that servicing notes through third party should be the preferred choice. This section has also established that the simple note servicing process has several advantages associated with it. By hiring a third party for note-servicing, both the buyer and seller can enjoy responsible, flexible personal service and customer care.

Chapter Eight

Want to Exit:

Learn How You Can Use Popular Exit Strategies

In many instances, there is a sole reason investors opt for non-performing bank notes: the wide array of exit strategies that can be used in the event the buyer needs to back out (whatever the reason). Given the recent economic meltdown, investors prefer to have an exit strategy in place. It is only obvious that they want to safeguard themselves against any scenarios that may jeopardize them financially. Whether it is about the inability to pay or a covenant breach, several exit strategies that ideally can suit any investor are outlined below.

1- Get note to re-perform and resell note

2- Work with the owner to sell the property, and receive full payoff or short sale payoff

3- Cash for keys/Deed in lieu

4- Refinance

5- Foreclosure

To go about the exit process effortlessly while using each of the strategies listed above, the information below provides instructions.

1- Get Note to Re-Perform and Resell Note

For those wondering how to transform a non-performing note into a performing one, the process is as follows.

The home-owner is contacted and efforts are made to make her/him agree on some sort of loan modification. This modification comes as better terms of agreement which could be anything from offering lower interest rates to principal reduction.

This strategy is not something out-of-the-box, as note-servicing companies such as BSI Financial Services (www.bsifinancial.com) have been using it for years now. Once the loan re-performs and has seasoned for one year, it can be sold to any investor dealing with performing notes. The best part is that, in most cases, this performing note is sold for an 80% or better principal balance.

2- Work with the Owner to Sell the Property and Receive Full Payoff or Short Sale Payoff

Another strategy involves working with the owner to sell the property. The owner either receives a short sale payoff or a full payoff. This depends on the amount for which the property is sold.

If the property is sold at a price higher than that of the loan amount, you receive a full payoff. If the property is sold for a price lower than that of the loan amount, it then classifies as a short sale. However, it will be a short sale pending on *your approval*.

3- Cash for Keys/Deed in Lieu

Cash for keys, also known as *deed in lieu*. Is yet another popular exit strategy used for non-performing bank notes. Essentially, this is accomplished when the note buyer offers the homeowner to walk away from the property by signing over the deed to her/him. The homeowner receives some sort of incentive in return.

For example, the note-buyer can offer the homeowner cash to have a fresh new start. This works in favor of both parties because the note buyer receives the property's title, and the homeowner can easily escape a foreclosure to keep her/his otherwise likely colorful record clean. All s/he has to do is simply walk away from an upside down property and he/she has practically nothing to lose.

4- Refinance

This is an exit strategy a lot of investors do not know exists. Recently, the federal government has introduced a program known as the Short Refinance

Program. Under this program, a borrower with an upside down mortgage will be allowed to refinance up to 97% of the value of the property provided that a lender is willing to accept principal reduction on the loan.

This is probably one of the most viable of all exit strategies and for good reasons. The homeowner is allowed to keep the home at easy mortgage terms. It is also the most profitable of all the exit strategies discussed so far.

5- Foreclosure

The foreclosure, in this case, is often referred to as a *friendly foreclosure*. Using foreclosure as an exit strategy is nothing new. It is often used for a home owner who cannot be located, is unyielding or is being plain unreasonable. This exit strategy is also used in case the homeowner is being unrealistic in demands and has her/his head in the sand.

In the event of a foreclosure, the note holder initiates the process by contacting an attorney in the specific county where the property is located. S/He may also contact the note-servicing company to accomplish the feat. Here, it is important to specify that the laws of foreclosure vary from one state to the other. They are subject to timelines as well.

To access comprehensive information regarding foreclosure, www.foreclosurelaw.org is a resource you can trust. This website can help you see a clear picture of how long the process may take. Bear in mind that only 40% to 50% of foreclosure cases initiated end up at foreclosures. This is because, in most of the cases, as soon as the foreclosure process begins, headstrong borrowers are forced to the negotiating table in an effort to avoid all of the hassle.

Chapter Nine

PET PEEVES

We have been fortunate in this business and in life. Once you get started in the Note business it is our experience that you don't stop after your first couple of Note deals. As you continue to grow you will come across situations and scenarios that may or may not make sense to you. Remember that all companies have different structures and capital limitations.

Some claims that you likely will come across in the business are: "I'm the authorized seller," "I own the notes," "I'm Bank Direct," etc... you get the idea. Most of the time, you'll find out that the broker or seller is actually not Bank Direct or even close!

Don't be that guy. Don't try to sell notes of which you have no real grasp of the deals... also known as "the internet guy."

You'll encounter similar claims with respect to the "buyer." For instance, you may hear individuals claiming to be the buyer or the principal. They also may claim to be fully funded; to have proof of funds; to be able to "buy into the millions;" to "only buy tapes;" etc. Don't be that guy either. Don't lie. *Be as honest as you can be and people will respect you, buyers and sellers alike.*

Afterword

Understand that your time is limited, so please don't waste it living someone else's life.

You already know what you truly want to become.

Don't let the others' opinions drown out your own inner voice.

When we started our journey, the first thing we did was to throw away all the expectations laid out by our friends, family and girlfriends.

When Apollo Financial Group began, it did not come with an instruction manual on how to become the number one note company in the nation. We had to figure that out every step of the way. With each new challenge and with each new market trend, everyone thought we would fail.

Through the fog and animosity from those around us --even those closest to us --we emerged as a world leader in the mortgage note business, and we are not done.

We didn't react against bad situations we merged with those situations instead.

Solutions always arise from the challenges.

What empowers us most is the real ability to help an American homeowner one note at a time.

The Final Word...For Now...

If you are looking for financial freedom, investing in non-performing bank notes can be the perfect option to carve your way out of economic insecurity. In order to have a productive four-hour work week model while enjoying the best of both worlds, setting up your own business is essential.

Synonymous with success, it allows for many benefits -- and what better opportunity to come your way than bank note investment?

Unlike other options that will demand sacrifices in the name of time, focus and discipline, investment in bank notes emerges as the perfect money-making opportunity, as it will not only generate passive income but also will help you achieve peace of mind. With minimal effort, you can finally realize your dreams.

There is no doubt that there are countless investment options available today. Non-performing bank loans, however, have an edge over all others because, perhaps, it is the only alternative where you can earn substantial profits with minimum risks.

Just imagine: Despite today's turbulent economy, you won't have to worry about post-retirement blues. You won't have to spend hours balancing your income and expenses each month. No longer will you have to spend sleepless nights wondering how you will make ends meet. When you deal in bank notes, you will end up with sufficient savings.

The great thing is that you do not have to be alone in this when trying to navigate this industry. Companies that already have the capital and network in place -- like Apollo Financial Group and Mortgage Float -- already exist. Streamlining the acquisition process, such companies can help you acquire non performing bank notes while steering clear of all the hassles.

The truth is, financial security is one of the biggest delights known to mankind. Knowing that you won't have to please a boss the next day and can still survive your chosen lifestyle is a blessing. Remember, either you work to fulfill your dreams or others will employ you to fulfill theirs. *The choice is yours.*

Financial freedom is something we all should strive for, and making money through bank notes is the most promising way to do it right. So, get down to business. It is time you secure enough cash to flash. It is time you start investing in bank notes.

Glossary

Affiliate Marketing - A type of performance-based marketing in which a business rewards one or more affiliates for each visitor or customer brought by the affiliate's own marketing efforts.

The industry has four core players: (1) the merchant (also known as 'retailer' or 'brand');(2) the network (that contains offers for the affiliate to choose from and also takes care of the payments);(3) the publisher (also known as "the affiliate"); and (4) the customer. The market has grown in complexity, resulting in the emergence of a secondary tier of players, including affiliate management agencies, super-affiliates and specialized third party vendors.

Affiliate marketing overlaps with other Internet marketing methods to some degree, because affiliates often use regular advertising methods. Those methods include organic search engine optimization (SEO), paid search engine marketing (Pay per Click,

PPC), e-mail marketing, content marketing and -- in some sense -- display advertising. On the other hand, affiliates sometimes use less orthodox techniques, such as publishing reviews of products or services offered by a partner.

Affiliate marketing is commonly confused with referral marketing, as both forms of marketing use third parties to drive sales to the retailer. However, both are distinct forms of marketing; the main difference between them being that affiliate marketing relies purely on financial motivations to drive sales while referral marketing relies on trust and personal relationships to drive sales.

Advertisers frequently overlook affiliate marketing. While search engines, e-mail, and website syndication capture much of the attention of online retailers, affiliate marketing carries a much lower profile. Still, affiliates continue to play a significant role in e-retailers' marketing strategies.

Amazon - The largest Internet-based retailer in the United States.

Amortization - When used in the context of a home purchase, this refers to the process by which loan principal decreases over the life of a loan, typically an amortizing loan. With each mortgage payment that is made, a portion of the payment is applied towards reducing the principal, and another portion of the payment is applied towards paying the interest on the loan.

An amortization schedule, a table detailing each periodic payment on a loan, shows this ratio of principal and interest and demonstrates how a loan's principal amount decreases over time. An amortization schedule can be generated by an amortization calculator. Negative amortization is an amortization schedule where the loan amount actually increases through not paying the full interest.

In common legal systems, amortization refers to a contract (or informally known as an agreement).

APOR - An annual percentage rate that is based on average interest rates, fees and other terms on mortgages offered to highly qualified borrowers. Your mortgage will be considered a higher-priced mortgage loan if the APR is a certain percentage higher than the **APOR,** depending on what type of loan you have.

Asset Inspection –This refers to the examination of an asset -- such as real estate property -- in order to determine its condition. Asset inspectors are industry experts who help identify the condition of the property and determine the cost of renovation.

Asset Management Team - Broadly defined, this term refers to any system that monitors and maintains things of value to an entity or group. It may apply to both tangible assets such as buildings and to intangible concepts such as intellectual property and goodwill. Asset management is a systematic process of deploying, operating, maintaining, upgrading, and disposing of assets cost-effectively.

The term is most commonly used in the financial world to describe people and companies that manage investments on behalf of others. These include, for example, investment managers that manage the assets of a pension fund.

Alternative views of asset management in the engineering environment are: the practice of managing assets to achieve the greatest return (particularly useful for productive assets such as plant and equipment), and the process of monitoring and maintaining facilities systems, with the objective of providing the best possible service to users (appropriate for public infrastructure assets).

Bank Notes – A piece of paper money, constituting a central bank's promissory note to pay a stated sum to the bearer on demand.

Best Price - The lowest price for which a buyer can buy something.

Bonds - A debt investment in which an investor loans money to an entity (typically corporate or governmental) for a defined period of time at a variable or fixed interest rate.

Bonds are used by companies, municipalities, states and sovereign governments to raise money and finance a variety of projects and activities. Owners of bonds are debt holders, or creditors, of the issuer.

A bond, therefore, is a form of loan or I.O.U. (sounded, "I owe you").The holder of the bond is the lender (creditor);the issuer of the bond is the borrower (debtor);and the coupon is the interest. Bonds provide the borrower with external funds to finance long-term investments, or, in the case of government bonds, to finance current expenditure. Certificates of deposit (CDs) or short term commercial paper are considered to be money market instruments and not bonds. The main difference is in the length of the term of the instrument.

Bonds and stocks are both securities, but the major difference between the two is that (capital) stockholders have an equity stake in the company (i.e. they are investors); whereas bondholders have a creditor stake in the company (i.e. they are lenders). Being a creditor, bondholders have absolute priority and will be repaid before stockholders (who are owners) in the event of bankruptcy. Another difference is that bonds usually have a defined term, or maturity, after which the bond is redeemed, whereas stocks are typically outstanding indefinitely. An exception is an irredeemable bond, such as Consols, which is a perpetuity --a bond with no maturity.

Broker - A person who buys and sells goods or assets for others.

Broker Price Opinion - BPO; The process used by a hired sales agent to determine the potential selling price or estimated value of a real estate property.

BPOs are popularly used in situations where a financial institution believes the expense and delay of an appraisal is unnecessary. The broker may do a drive-by BPO or an interior BPO. In drive-by BPOs, the professionals do not have access to the interior of the property; they rely on exterior appearance, neighborhood information, comparables, and other documentation.

The interior BPO is more in-depth; it requires advanced contact with the property's inhabitants, evaluation of the interior and exterior, measuring to verify rooms and dimensions and additional photographs.

Bullish Trend - An upward trend in the prices of an industry's stocks or the overall rise in broad market indices.

In other words, a bull market is a period of generally rising prices. The start of a bull market is generally marked by widespread pessimism. This crucial moment is when the *crowd* is the most *bearish*. The feeling of despondency changes to hope, "optimism" and eventually euphoria. This is often leading the economic cycle, for example in a full recession, or earlier.

Cash Flow - Cash flow is the movement of money into or out of a business, project, or financial product. It is usually measured during a specified, limited period of time. Measurement of cash flow can be used for calculating other parameters that give information on a company's value and situation:

- To determine a project's rate of return or value. The time of cash flows into and out of projects are used as inputs in financial models such as internal rate of return and net present value.

- To determine problems with a business's liquidity. Being profitable does not necessarily mean being liquid. A company can fail because of a shortage of cash even while profitable.

- As an alternative measure of a business's profits when it is believed that accrual accounting concepts do not represent economic realities. For instance, a company may be notionally profitable but generating little operational cash (as may be the case for a company that barters its products rather than selling for cash). In such a case, the company may be deriving additional operating cash by issuing shares or raising additional debt finance.

- Cash flow can be used to evaluate the 'quality' of income generated by accrual accounting. When net income is composed of large non-cash items it is considered low quality.

- To evaluate the risks within a financial product; For instance, matching cash requirements, evaluating default risk, re-investment requirements, etc.

Cash flow notion is based loosely on cash flow statement accounting standards. The term is flexible and can refer to time intervals spanning over past-future. It can refer to the total of all flows involved or a subset of those flows. Subset terms include net cash flow, operating cash flow and free cash flow.

Certificate of Deposits - (CD) A time deposit; A financial product commonly sold in the United States and elsewhere by banks, thrift institutions, and credit unions.

CDs are similar to savings accounts in that they are insured and thus are virtually risk free; they are "money in the bank." In the USA, CDs are insured by the Federal Deposit Insurance Corporation (FDIC) for banks and by the National Credit Union Administration (NCUA) for credit unions. They are different from savings accounts in that the CD has a specific, fixed term (often monthly, three months, six months, or one to five years) and, usually, a fixed interest rate.

Classified Ad - An advertisement in a newspaper, magazine, or the like generally dealing with offers of or requests for jobs, houses, apartments, used cars, etc.

Clean Title of Property - This is the phrase used to state that the owner of real property owns it free and clear of encumbrances. In a more limited sense, it is used to state that, although the owner does not own clear title, it is nevertheless within the power of the owner to convey clear title.

For example, a property may be encumbered by a mortgage. This encumbrance means that no one has clear title to the property. However, standard terms in a mortgage require the mortgage holder to release the mortgage if a certain amount of money is paid. Therefore, a buyer with enough money to satisfy both the mortgage and the current owner can obtain clear title.

Closing Costs - Fees paid at the closing of a real estate transaction. This point in time, called *the closing*, is when the title to the property is transferred to the buyer. Closing costs are incurred by either the buyer or the seller. Closing costs include attorney's fees; survey fee; brokerage commission; recording fees; title service cost; document or transaction stamps or taxes; mortgage application fees; appraisal fees; prepaid insurance; inspection fees; property taxes; homeowner association dues; pro-rate interest; etc.

Collateral (Loan) - A borrower's pledge of specific property to a lender, to secure repayment of a loan. The collateral serves as protection for a lender against a borrower's default. In other words, it can be used to offset the loan to any borrower failing to pay the principal and interest under the terms of a loan obligation. If a borrower does default on a loan (due to insolvency or other event), that borrower forfeits (gives up) the property pledged as collateral, with the lender then becoming the owner of the property.

Colorful Credit History - Responsible repayment of loan amount.

Commercial Property - Commercial property includes office buildings, industrial property, medical centers, hotels, malls, retail stores, farm land, multifamily housing buildings, warehouses and garages. In many states, residential property containing more than a certain number of units qualifies as commercial property for borrowing and tax purposes.

Commodity - A raw material or primary agricultural product that can be bought and sold, such as gold, copper or coffee. The exact definition of the term commodity is specifically used to describe a class of goods for which there is demand, but which is supplied without qualitative differentiation across a market.

One of the characteristics of a commodity good is that its price is determined as a function of its market as a whole. Well-established physical commodities have actively traded spot and derivative markets. Generally, these are basic resources and agricultural products such as iron ore, crude oil, coal, salt, sugar, tea, coffee beans, soybeans, aluminum, copper, rice, wheat, gold, silver, palladium, and platinum. Soft commodities are goods that are grown, while hard commodities are ones that are extracted through mining.

Competitive Prices - A price that is below or on par with the market price.

Conventional Financing - A conventional loan or financing option is any loan which is not guaranteed or insured by the federal government. The loans are held in the lender's investment portfolio until they are either paid in full or foreclosed upon.

Costly Makeover - Repairs/renovations that will require a significant amount of money to carry out and complete.

Craigslist - Craigslist is a classified advertisements website with sections devoted to jobs, housing, personals, for sale, items wanted, services etc.

Credit Report - This document is compiled to let lenders know your credit history. The report contains your credit score, which is a numerical expression based on a level analysis of the past credit history, to represent creditworthiness of the person. A credit score is primarily based on credit report information typically sourced from credit bureaus.

Lenders, such as banks and credit card companies, use credit scores to evaluate the potential risk posed by lending money to consumers and to mitigate losses due to bad debt. Lenders use credit scores to determine who qualifies for a loan, at what interest rate, and what credit limits. Lenders also use credit scores to determine which customers are likely to bring in the most revenue. The use of credit or identity scoring prior to authorizing access or granting credit is an implementation of a trusted system.

The use of credit scores is not limited to banks. Other organizations, such as mobile phone companies, insurance companies, landlords and government departments employ the same techniques. Credit scoring also has much overlap with data mining, which uses many similar techniques. These techniques combine thousands of factors but are similar or identical.

There are different methods of calculating credit scores. FICO score, the most widely known type of credit score, is a credit score developed by FICO, previously known as Fair Isaac Corporation. It is used by many mortgage lenders that use a risk-based system to determine the possibility that the borrower may default on financial obligations to the mortgage lender. All credit scores must be subject to availability. The credit bureaus all have their own credit scores: Equifax's ScorePower (FICO score from Equifax), Equifax Credit Score, Experian's PLUS score, and TransUnion's credit score, and each also sells the VantageScore credit score. In addition, many large lenders, including the major credit card issuers, have developed their own proprietary scoring models.

FICO is a measure of past ability to pay. New credit scores that focus more on future ability to pay are being deployed to enhance credit risk models. New credit scores have been developed in the last decade by companies such as Scorelogix, PRBC, L2C, Innovis etc. that do not use bureau data to predict creditworthiness. Scorelogix's JSS Credit Score uses a different set of risk factors --such as the borrower's job stability, income, income sufficiency, and impact of economy --in predicting credit risk; the use of such alternative credit scores is on the rise. These new types of credit scores are often combined with FICO or bureau scores to improve the accuracy of predictions. Most lenders today use some combination of bureau scores and alternative credit scores to develop better understanding of a borrower's ability to pay.

Americans are entitled to one free credit report in every 12-month period from each of the three credit bureaus, but are not entitled to receive a free credit score. The three credit bureaus run www.annualcreditreport.com, where users can get their free credit reports. Credit scores are available as an add-on feature of the report for a fee. This fee is usually $7.95, as the FTC regulates this charge, and the credit bureaus are not allowed to charge an exorbitant fee for their credit score. If the consumer disputes an item on a credit report obtained using the free system, under the Fair Credit Reporting Act (FCRA), the credit bureaus have 45 days to investigate, rather than 30 days for reports obtained otherwise.

Alternatively, consumers wishing to obtain their credit scores can, in some cases, purchase them separately from the credit bureaus or can purchase their FICO score directly from FICO. Credit scores (including FICO scores) are also made available free by subscription to one of the many credit report monitoring services available from the credit bureaus or other third parties, although to actually obtain the scores gratis from most such services, one must use a credit card to sign up for a free trial subscription of the service and then cancel before the first monthly charge.

Currency Notes - A generally accepted form of money, including coins and paper notes, which is issued by a government and circulated within an economy.

Customer Demand - Customer demand is the utility for a good or service of an economic agent, relative to his/her income.

Deed in Lieu (of Foreclosure) - This is a deed instrument in which a mortgagor (the borrower) conveys all interest in a real property to the mortgagee (the lender) in order to satisfy a loan that is in default and therefore avoid foreclosure proceedings.

The deed in lieu of foreclosure offers several advantages to both the borrower and the lender. The main advantage to the borrower is that it immediately releases her/him from most or all of the personal indebtedness associated with the defaulted loan. The borrower also avoids the public notoriety of a foreclosure proceeding and may receive more generous terms than s/he would in a formal foreclosure. Another benefit to the borrower is that it hurts her/his credit less than a foreclosure does.

Advantages to a lender include a reduction in the time and cost of a repossession; lower risk of borrower revenge (metal theft and vandalism of the property before sheriff eviction); and additional advantages if the borrower subsequently files for bankruptcy.

If there are any junior liens a deed in lieu is a less attractive option for the lender. The lender will likely not want to assume the liability of the junior liens from the property owner, and accordingly, the lender will prefer to foreclose in order to clean the title.

In order to be considered a deed in lieu of foreclosure, the indebtedness must be secured by the real estate being transferred. Both sides must enter into the transaction voluntarily and in good faith. The settlement agreement must have total consideration that is at least equal to the fair market value of the property being conveyed. Sometimes, the lender will not proceed with a deed in lieu of foreclosure if the outstanding indebtedness of the borrower exceeds the current fair value of the property. Other times, lenders will agree since they will end up with the property anyway and the foreclosure process is costly to the lender.

Deed of Trust - In real estate in the United States, a deed of trust (also known as a trust deed) is a document wherein legal title in real property is transferred to a trustee, which holds it as security for a loan (debt) between a borrower and lender. The equitable title remains with the borrower. The borrower is referred to as the trustor, while the lender is referred to as the beneficiary.

Default (Property) - A default in a real estate contract happens when one party to the contract fails to fulfill the terms of the agreement. It is not a crime to be in default of a real estate contract. However, the party found to be in default can be sued in court for failure to perform and for damages resulting from defaulting. Default of a real estate contract is also called "material breach of contract" or "breach of contract." Contract law states that a material breach of contract is an irreparable break in a legally binding contract.

Defaulted Loans - Default is a failure to meet the legal obligations (or conditions) of a loan, for example when a home buyer fails to make a mortgage payment or when a corporation or government fails to pay a bond which has reached maturity.

Delinquent/Bad Debts - An amount owed by a debtor that is unlikely to be paid due, for example, to a company going into liquidation. There are various technical definitions of what constitutes a bad debt, depending on accounting conventions, regulatory treatment and the institution provisioning. In the United States, bank loans with more than ninety days' arrears become *problem loans*. Accounting sources advise that the full amount of a bad debt be written off to the profit and loss account or a provision for bad debts as soon as it is foreseen.

Doubtful debts are those debts which a business or individual is unlikely to be able to collect. The reasons for potential non-payment can include disputes over supply, delivery, the condition of item or the appearance of financial stress within a customer's operations. When such a dispute occurs, it is prudent to add this debt or portion thereof to the doubtful debt reserve. This is done to avoid over-stating the assets of the business as trade debtors are reported net of doubtful debt. When there is no longer any doubt that a debt is uncollectible, the debt becomes bad.

For instance, an example of a debt becoming uncollectible would be as follows: Once final payments have been made from the liquidation of a customer's limited liability company, no further action can be taken.

Also known as a *bad debt reserve*, this label is a contra account listed within the current asset section of the balance sheet. The doubtful debt reserve holds a sum of money to allow a reduction in the accounts receivable ledger due to non-collection of debts. This can also be referred to as an allowance for bad debts. Once a doubtful debt becomes uncollectable, the amount will be written off.

Delinquent/Bad Debts - An amount owed by a debtor that is unlikely to be paid due, for example, to a company going into liquidation. There are various technical definitions of what constitutes a bad debt, depending on accounting conventions, regulatory treatment and the institution provisioning. In the United States, bank loans with more than ninety days' arrears become *problem loans*. Accounting sources advise that the full amount of a bad debt be written off to the profit and loss account or a provision for bad debts as soon as it is foreseen.

Doubtful debts are those debts which a business or individual is unlikely to be able to collect. The reasons for potential non-payment can include disputes over supply, delivery, the condition of item or the appearance of financial stress within a customer's operations. When such a dispute occurs, it is prudent to add this debt or portion thereof to the doubtful debt reserve. This is done to avoid overstating the assets of the business as trade debtors are reported net of doubtful debt. When there is no longer any doubt that a debt is uncollectible, the debt becomes bad.

For instance, an example of a debt becoming uncollectible would be as follows: Once final payments have been made from the liquidation of a customer's limited liability company, no further action can be taken.

Also known as a *bad debt reserve*, this label is a contra account listed within the current asset section of the balance sheet. The doubtful debt reserve holds a sum of money to allow a reduction in the accounts receivable ledger due to non-collection of debts. This can also be referred to as an allowance for bad debts. Once a doubtful debt becomes uncollectable, the amount will be written off.

(Real Estate) Developers - Also known as property developers, they take on in multifaceted a business, encompassing activities that range from the renovation and re-lease of existing buildings to the purchase of raw land and the sale of improved land or parcels to others. Real estate development is different from construction, although many developers also construct.

Discount (Loan) - A deduction from the usual cost of something, typically given for prompt or advance payment or to a special category of buyers.

eBay - eBay is an American multinational corporation and e-commerce company, providing consumer to consumer as well as business to consumer sales services via Internet.

Economic Condition - The state of the economy in a country or region.

The term *economic cycle* (or *business cycle* or *boom–bust cycle*) refers to aggregate production, trade and activity over several months or years in a market economy. The economic cycle is the downward and upward movement of levels of gross domestic product (GDP) and refers to the period of expansions and contractions in the level of economic activities (business fluctuations) around its long-term growth trend.

These fluctuations also typically involve shifts over time between periods of relatively rapid economic growth (an expansion or boom) and periods of relative stagnation or decline (a contraction or recession).

Economic cycles are usually measured by considering the growth rate of real GDP. Despite being termed cycles, these fluctuations in economic activity can prove unpredictable.

Economic Meltdown - An economic meltdown is a business cycle contraction. It is a general slowdown in economic activity. Macroeconomic indicators such as gross domestic product (GDP), investment spending; capacity utilization; household income; business profits; and inflation fall, while bankruptcies and the unemployment rate rise. There is no precise definition of an economic collapse. The term has been used to describe a broad range of bad economic conditions, ranging from a severe, prolonged depression with high bankruptcy rates and high unemployment (such as the Great Depression of the 1930s), to a breakdown in normal commerce caused by hyperinflation (such as in Weimar Germany in the 1920s), or even an economically-caused sharp increase in the death rate -- and perhaps even a decline in population (such as in countries of the former USSR in the 1990s).

Estimated Market Value - Also known as Open Market Valuation(OMV), it is the price at which an asset would trade in a competitive auction setting. Market value is often used interchangeably with open market value, fair value or fair market value, although these terms have distinct definitions in different standards, and may differ in some circumstances.

Existing Dollar Value - In real estate, property values are not the same as property prices. Property value is an estimate of what a home or a piece of land is actually worth; the price may be higher or lower, depending on who has the best bargaining skills.

Exit Strategy - An exit strategy is a means of leaving one's current situation, either after a predetermined objective has been achieved, or as a strategy to mitigate failure. In entrepreneurship and strategic management, an exit strategy or exit plan is a way to transition the ownership of a company to another company (e.g. through a merger or acquisition) or to investors (e.g. through an initial public offering). Other types of exit strategy include management buyouts or employee buyouts (common in the manufacturing industry).

Transition companies are professional mergers and acquisitions companies that assist business owners with their exit strategy. Services offered are often referred to as transition management services.

Fair Price of Property – Also known as Fair Market Value (FMV), it is an estimate of the market value of a property, based on what a knowledgeable, willing and unpressured buyer would probably pay to a knowledgeable, willing, and unpressured seller in the market. An estimate of fair market value may be founded either on precedent or extrapolation. Fair market value differs from the intrinsic value that an individual may place on the same asset based on their own preferences and circumstances

Financial Expert - A person who has years of experience in giving advice to people on how to manage and grow their finances.

Financial Freedom - Also known as *financial independence*, the term is generally used to describe the state of having sufficient personal wealth to live, without having to work actively for basic necessities. For financially independent people, their assets generate income that is greater than their expenses. It does not matter how old or young someone is or how much money they have or make. If they can generate enough money to meet their needs from sources other than their primary occupation, then they have achieved financial independence.

Age is potentially irrelevant with respect to financial independence. If they are 25 years old and their expenses are only $100 per month, and they posess assets that generate $101 or more per month, they have achieved financial independence. They are now free to do things that they enjoy without having to worry as much – even if they only cost $1.

If, on the other hand, they are 50 years old and earn $1 million dollars per month but still have expenses above $1million dollars per month, then they are *not* financially independent because they still must generate the difference each month just to stay even. However, this needs to take into consideration the effects of inflation.

If a person needs $100/month for living expenses today, that figure will be $105/month next year and $110.25/month in the following year to support the same lifestyle assuming a 5% annual inflation rate. Therefore, if the person in the above example obtains their passive income from a perpetuity, there will be a time when they lose their financial independence because of inflation.

Financial Institution - In financial economics, a financial institution is an institution that provides financial services for its clients or members.

Financial Objectives: Goals related to returns that a firm will strive to accomplish during the period covered by its financial plan.

Financial Security – Also referred to as *economic security*, this is the condition of having stable income or other resources to support a standard of living now and in the foreseeable future. It includes:

- probable continued solvency;
- predictability of the future cash flow of a person or other economic entity, such as a country; and
- employment security or job security.

Financial security more often refers to individual and family money management and savings. *Economic security* tends to include the broader effect of a society's production levels and monetary support for non-working citizens.

Financial System - The financial system is the system that allows the transfer of money between savers and borrowers. A financial system can operate on a global, regional or firm-specific level.

Foreclosed Homes - A foreclosed home is one in which the owner is unable to make his mortgage loan payments, and the bank therefore repossessed the home.

These homes are usually not for sale until the entire foreclosure process is complete, and the bank lists the home in the local Multiple Listing Service (MLS).

Foreclosure - A legal process in which a lender attempts to recover the balance of a loan from a borrower who has stopped making payments to the lender by forcing the sale of the asset used as the collateral for the loan.

Formally, a mortgage lender (mortgagee), or other lien holder, obtains a termination of a mortgage borrower's (mortgagor's) equitable right of redemption, either by court order or by operation of law (after following a specific statutory procedure).

Usually a lender obtains a security interest from a borrower who mortgages or pledges an asset like a house to secure the loan. If the borrower defaults and the lender tries to repossess the property, courts of equity can grant the borrower the equitable right of redemption if the borrower repays the debt.

While this equitable right exists, it is a cloud on title, and the lender cannot be sure that they can successfully repossess the property. Therefore, through the process of foreclosure, the lender seeks to foreclose (in other words, *immediately terminate*) the equitable right of redemption, and take both legal and equitable title to the property in fee simple. Other lien holders can also foreclose the owner's right of redemption for other debts, such as for overdue taxes, unpaid contractors' bills or overdue homeowners' association dues or assessments.

The foreclosure process as applied to *residential* mortgage loans is a bank or other secured creditor selling or repossessing a parcel of real property after the owner has failed to comply with an agreement between the lender and borrower called a *mortgage* or *deed of trust*. Commonly, the violation of the mortgage is a default in payment of a promissory note, secured by a lien on the property. When the process is complete, the lender can sell the property and keep the proceeds to pay off its mortgage and any legal costs, and it is typically said that *the lender has foreclosed its mortgage or lien.*

If the promissory note was made with a recourse clause, and if the sale does not bring enough to pay the existing balance of principal and fees, the mortgagee can file a claim for a deficiency judgment. In many states in the United States, items included to calculate the amount of a deficiency judgment include the loan principal, accrued interest and attorney fees less the amount the lender bid at the foreclosure sale.

The mortgage holder can usually initiate foreclosure at a time specified in the mortgage documents, typically some period of time after a default condition occurs. Within the United States, Canada and many other countries, several types of foreclosure exist. In the United States, two of them -- namely, by judicial sale and by power of sale -- are widely used, but other modes of foreclosure are also possible in a few states.

Foreclosure Auction - When the entity auctions a foreclosed property (in the United States, the entity is typically a county sheriff or designee), the note holder may set the starting price as the remaining balance on the mortgage loan. There are, however, a number of issues that affect how pricing for properties is considered, including bankruptcy rulings. In a weak market, the foreclosing party may set the starting price at a lower amount if it believes the real estate securing the loan is worth less than the remaining principal of the loan. Time from notice of foreclosures to actual property sales is dependent on many factors such method of foreclosure (judicial or non-judicial).

In the case where the remaining mortgage balance is higher than the actual home value the foreclosing party is unlikely to attract auction bids at this price level. A house that has gone through a foreclosure auction and failed to attract any acceptable bids may remain the property of the owner of the mortgage. That inventory is called REO (Real-Estate Owned). In these situations, the owner/servicer tries to sell it through standard real estate channels.

Form 1098 – This is an IRS tax form, also known as the *Mortgage Interest Statement*, used to report interest that a taxpayer has paid on his or her mortgage. Such interest may be tax-deductible as an itemized deduction.

Generally speaking, tax forms are used for taxpayers and tax-exempt organizations to report financial information to the Internal Revenue Service (IRS) of the United States. They are used to report income, calculate taxes to be paid to the federal government of the United States, and disclose other information as required by the Internal Revenue Code (IRC). There are over 800 various forms and schedules.

Franchise - An authorization granted by a government or company to an individual or group enabling them to carry out specified commercial activities (e.g. providing a broadcasting service or acting as an agent for a company's products).

Further Borrower's Obligations – The mortgagor may be required to pay for Private Mortgage Insurance (PMI), for as long as the principal of his or her primary mortgage is above 80% of the value of his or her property. In most situations, insurance requirements are sufficient to guarantee that the lender gets some pre-defined percentage of the loan value back, either from foreclosure auction proceeds or from PMI or a combination thereof.

Nevertheless, in an illiquid real estate market or following a significant drop in real estate prices, it may happen that the property being foreclosed is sold for less than the remaining balance on the primary mortgage loan, and there may be no insurance to cover the loss. In this case, the court overseeing the foreclosure process may enter a deficiency judgment against the mortgagor. Deficiency judgments can be used to place a lien on the borrower's other property that obligates the mortgagor to repay the difference. It gives the lender a legal right to collect the remainder of debt out of mortgagor's other assets (if any).

There are exceptions to this rule, however. If the mortgage is a non-recourse debt (which is often the case with owner-occupied residential mortgages in the United States.), the lender may not go after the borrower's assets to recuperate his/her losses. The lender's ability to pursue deficiency judgment may be restricted by state laws. In California and some other states, original mortgages (the ones taken out at the time of purchase) are typically non-recourse loans; however, refinanced loans and home equity lines of credit are not.

If the lender chooses not to pursue deficiency judgment -- or cannot because the mortgage is non-recourse -- and writes off the loss, the borrower may have to pay income taxes on the un-repaid amount if it can be considered *forgiven debt*. Recent changes in tax laws, though, may change the way these amounts are reported.

Any liens resulting from other loans taken out against the property being foreclosed (second mortgages, HELOCs) are wiped out, so to speak, by foreclosure, but the borrower is still obligated to pay those loans off if they are not paid out of the foreclosure auction's proceeds.

Because the right of redemption is an equitable right, foreclosure is an action in equity. To keep the right of redemption, the debtor may be able to petition the court for an injunction. If repossession is imminent, the debtor must seek a temporary restraining order. However, the debtor may have to post a bond in the amount of the debt. This protects the creditor if the attempt to stop foreclosure is simply an attempt to escape the debt.

Gold Investment - Investors generally invest in gold as a way of diversifying risk. The gold market is subject to speculation, as are other markets, especially through the use of futures contracts and derivatives.

Holding Cost (Real Estate) - The expenditure to keep and maintain a property. The most obvious holding costs include rent for the required space; equipment, materials, and labor to operate the space; insurance; security; and other direct expenses.

Home-based business - A home business (HBB) is a small business that operates from the business owner's home office. In addition to location, home businesses are usually defined by having a very small number of employees, usually all immediate family of the business owner, in which case it is also a family business.

Investment – An amount of money put into something for profit or material result.

Investment Portfolio - A hands-off or passive investment of securities in a portfolio.

A portfolio investment is made with the expectation of earning a return on it. This expected return is directly correlated with the investment's expected risk. Portfolio investment is distinct from direct investment, which involves taking a sizeable stake in a target company and possibly being involved with its day-to-day management.

IRS Lien - A lien imposed by law upon a property to secure the payment of taxes.

IRS Reporting: Tax information reporting in the United States is a requirement for organizations to report wage and non-wage payments made in the course of their trade or business to the Internal Revenue

Service (IRS). This area of government reporting and corporate responsibility is continuously growing, carrying with it a large number of regulatory requirements established by the federal government and the states. There are currently more than 30 types of tax information returns required by the federal government, and they provide the primary cross-checking measure the IRS has to verify accuracy of tax returns filed by individual taxpayers. Remember that Form 1099-S reports income from the sale of real estate.

Judgment Lien - A lien on a debtor's property that is granted to a creditor by court judgment.

Judicial Foreclosure - *Foreclosure by judicial sale*, more commonly known as *judicial foreclosure* -- available in every state (and required in many) -- involves the sale of the mortgaged property under the supervision of a court, with the proceeds going first to satisfy the mortgage; then other lien holders; and, finally, the mortgagor/borrower if any proceeds are left.

Under this system, the lender initiates foreclosure by filing a lawsuit against the borrower. As with all other legal actions, all parties must be notified of the foreclosure, but notification requirements vary significantly from state to state. A judicial decision is announced after the exchange of pleadings at a (usually short) hearing in a state or local court. In some rather rare instances, foreclosures are filed in federal courts.

Leasing of Property - A lease is a contract between an owner and a user of property.

In business lease agreements, the owner (lesser) receives financial compensation, and in exchange, the tenant (lessee) is given the right to operate his or her business on the property.

Legally Binding Document - A legally binding document is a document that is enforceable in a court of law. Generally, it requires signatures from the parties to the agreement and may need to be notarized depending on the document. In order to be legally binding, the agreement must be legal. A court will not enforce an agreement between parties that involves some illegal act no matter how carefully the document was drafted ad executed.

Legally Binding Document (Contract) - In common law legal systems, a contract (or informally known as an agreement in some jurisdictions) is an agreement having a lawful object entered into voluntarily by two or more parties, each of whom intends to create one or more legal obligations between them. The elements of a contract are *offer* and *acceptance* by *competent persons* having legal capacity who exchange *consideration* to create *mutuality of obligation.*

Lien - Lien is a form of security interest granted over an item of property to secure the payment of a debt or performance of some other obligation. The owner of the property, who grants the lien, is referred to as the lienee and the person who has the benefit of the lien is referred to as the lienor or lien holder.

Loan Modification - It is a process where the terms of a mortgage are modified outside the original terms of the contract agreed to by the lender (*mortgagee*) and borrower (*mortgagor*). In general, any loan can be modified, and the general process is referred to as loan modification or debt rescheduling.

Mortgages are modified to the benefit of the borrower in one or more of the following ways:

- Reduction in interest rate, or a change from a floating to a fixed rate, or in how the floating rate is computed;

- Reduction in principal;

- Reduction in the monthly payment;

- Reduction in late fees or other penalties;

- Lengthening of the loan term;

- Capping the monthly payment to a percentage of household income; or

- Mortgage forbearance program.

The borrower can be current, late, in default, in bankruptcy, or in foreclosure at the time the application for modification is made. The programs available will vary accordingly.

There may be modifications made at the discretion of the lender. The lender is motivated to offer better terms to the borrower because of the expectation that the borrower might be able to afford a lower payment, and that a performing loan (i.e. one in which payments are current) will be more valuable ultimately than the proceeds obtained from a foreclosure sale.

The state and federal government may structure a mortgage modification program as voluntary on the part of the lender, but may provide incentives for the lender to participate. A mandatory mortgage modification program requires the lender to modify mortgages meeting the criteria with respect to the borrower, the property and the loan payment history.

Lump Sum Amount - A lump sum is a single payment of money, as opposed to a series of payments made over time (such as an annuity).

Major Rework - Requires lots of repairs.

Mainstream Business - A traditional brick and mortar business that relies on face-to-face transactions with physical documents and physical currency or credit.

Maintenance Cost - The expenditures to fix or upkeep any sort of mechanical, plumbing or electrical device in a home. Home maintenance are of two types: Routine maintenance -- undertaken to keep the property items in good working condition -- and preventive maintenance -- to prevent trouble from arising.

Market Conditions - Features of the marketplace including interest rates, employment levels, demographics, vacancy rates, and absorption.

Market Trend - A market trend is a tendency of financial markets to move in a particular direction over time. These trends are classified as secular for long time frames; primary for medium time frames; and secondary for short time frames. Traders identify market trends using technical analysis, a framework which characterizes market trends as predictable price tendencies within the market when price reaches support and resistance levels, varying over time. Strictly, a trend can only be determined in hindsight, since at any time prices in the future are not known. This does not prevent people from prognosticating about future trends. Some people ascribe trends to pareidolia. The terms *bull market* and *bear market* describe upward and downward market trends, respectively, and can be used to describe either the market as a whole or specific sectors and securities.

Mass Mail Marketing - Mass mail marketing refers to directly marketing a commercial message to a group of people using paper and/or digital mail. Mass marketing is a market coverage strategy in which a firm decides to ignore market segment differences and appeal to the whole market with one offer or one strategy.

The idea is to broadcast a message that will reach the largest number of people possible. Traditionally, mass marketing has focused on radio, television and newspapers as the media used to reach this broad audience. By reaching the largest audience possible exposure to the product is maximized. In theory, this would directly correlate with a larger number of sales or buys into the product.

Measurable Period of Time - Within reasonable time; an amount of time that can be calculated relative to what it is you are attempting to obtain/accomplish.

Mechanic Lien - Mechanic's lien is a security interest in the title to property for the benefit of those who have supplied labor or materials that improve the property. The lien exists for both real property and personal property. In the realm of real estate property, it is called by various names including, generically, *construction lien*. It is also called a *material man's lien* or *supplier's lien* when referring to those supplying materials; a *laborer's lien* when referring to those supplying labor; and a *design professional's lien* when referring to architects or designers who contribute to a work of improvement. In the realm of personal property, it is also called an *artisan's lien*.

Mineral Deposits - Areas where an aggregate of a mineral is in an unusually high concentration.

Mortgage Note - In the United States, a mortgage note (also known as a real estate lien note or borrower's note) is a promissory note secured by a specified mortgage loan; it is a written promise to repay a specified sum of money plus interest at a specified rate and length of time to fulfill the promise.

Mortgage Payment - A regularly scheduled payment which includes principal and interest paid by borrower to lender of home loan.

Mutual Fund - An investment program funded by shareholders that trade in diversified holdings and is professionally managed.

Mutual funds are operated by money managers, who invest the fund's capital and attempt to produce capital gains and income for the fund's investors. A mutual fund's portfolio is structured and maintained to match the investment objectives stated in its prospectus.

In the United States, mutual funds must be registered with the U.S. Securities and Exchange Commission (the SEC), overseen by a board of directors and/or board of trustees, and managed by a Registered Investment Advisor. Mutual funds are also subject to an extensive and detailed regulatory regime set forth in the Investment Company Act of 1940. Mutual funds are not taxed on their income and profits if they comply with certain requirements under the U.S. Internal Revenue Code.

Mutual funds have both advantages and disadvantages compared to direct investing in individual securities. Today they play an important role in household finances, most notably in retirement planning.

There are three types of U.S. mutual funds—open-end funds, unit investment trusts, and closed-end funds. Open-end funds, the most common type, must be willing to buy back shares from investors every business day. Exchange-traded funds (ETFs) are open-end funds or unit investment trusts that trade on an exchange. Non-exchange traded open-end funds are most common, but ETFs have been gaining in popularity.

Mutual funds are generally classified by their principal investments. The four main categories of funds are money market funds; bond or fixed income funds; stock or equity funds; and hybrid funds. Funds may also be categorized as index (or passively managed) or actively managed. Investors in a mutual fund pay the fund's expenses, which reduce the fund's returns and performance. There is controversy about the level of these expenses.

Non-judicial Foreclosure - *Foreclosure by power of sale*, also known as *non-judicial foreclosure*, is authorized by many states if a power of sale clause is included in the mortgage or if a deed of trust with such a clause was used, instead of an actual mortgage.

In some states, like California and Texas, nearly all so-called mortgages are actually deeds of trust. This process involves the sale of the property by the mortgage holder without court supervision (as elaborated upon below). This process is generally much faster and cheaper than foreclosure by judicial sale.

As in judicial sale, the mortgage holder and other lien holders are respectively first and second claimants to the proceeds from the sale.

Non-Performing Assets - NPA; A credit facility in which the interest and/or installment of principal has remained past due for a specified period of time. NPA is used by financial institutions that refer to loans that are in jeopardy of default. Once the borrower has failed to make interest or principle payments for 90 days, the loan is considered to be a non-performing asset.

Non-performing assets are problematic for financial institutions since they depend on interest payments for income. Troublesome pressure from the economy can lead to a sharp increase in non-performing loans and often results in massive write-downs.

With a view to moving towards international best practices and to ensure greater transparency, it had been decided to adopt the *90 days overdue* norm for identification of NPA, from the year ending March 31, 2004. Accordingly, with effect from March 31, 2004, a non-performing asset (NPA) is a loan or an advance where:

- Interest and/or installment of principal remain overdue for a period of more than 90 days in respect of a term loan;

- The account remains 'out of order' for a period of more than 90 days, in respect of an Overdraft/Cash Credit (OD/CC);

- The bill remains overdue for a period of more than 90 days in the case of bills purchased and discounted;

- Interest and/or installment of principal remains overdue for two harvest seasons but for a period not exceeding two half years in the case of an advance granted for agricultural purposes;

- Any amount to be received remains overdue for a period of more than 90 days in respect of other accounts;

- Non-submission of Stock Statements for 3 Continuous Quarters in case of Cash Credit Facility; and

- No active transactions in the account (Cash Credit/Over Draft/EPC/PCFC) for more than 91days.

Non-Performing Loans - A loan is non-performing when payments of interest and principal are past due by 90 days or more, or at least 90 days of interest payments have been capitalized, refinanced or delayed by agreement, or payments are less than 90 days overdue, but there are other good reasons to doubt that payments will be made in full.

By bank regulatory definition non-performing loans consist of:

- other real estate owned which is taken by foreclosure or a deed in lieu of foreclosure;

- loans that are 90 days or more past due and still accruing interest; and

- loans which have been placed on nonaccrual (i.e., loans for which interest is no longer accrued and posted to the income statement).

Oil Reserves - Oil reserves are the amount of technically and economically recoverable oil.

OnlineAuctions - An auction that is held on the Internet.

Online auctions come in many different formats, but most popularly they are ascending English auctions; descending Dutch auctions; first-price sealed-bid; Vickrey auctions; or sometimes even a combination of multiple auctions, taking elements of one and forging them with another. The scope and reach of these auctions have been propelled by the Internet to a level beyond what the initial purveyors had anticipated. This is mainly because online auctions break down and remove the physical limitations of traditional auctions such as geography, presence, time, space, and a small target audience.

Outstanding Property Taxes - Property taxes that are unpaid by the homeowner.

Passive Income - Monies received on a regular basis, with little effort required to maintain it. It is closely related to the concept of *unearned income.*

> The American Internal Revenue Service categorizes income into three broad types: active (earned) income, passive (unearned) income, and portfolio income. It defines passive income as only coming from two sources: rental activity or "trade or business activities in which you do not materially participate." Other financial and government institutions also recognize it as an income obtained as a result of capital growth or in relation to negative gearing. Passive income is usually taxable.

Portfolio Managers - This can be either a person who makes investment decisions using money other people have placed under his or her control or a person who manages a financial institution's asset and liability (loan and deposit) portfolios. On the investments side, they work with a team of analysts and researchers and are ultimately responsible for establishing an investment strategy, selecting appropriate investments, and allocating each investment properly for a fund- or asset-management vehicle.

Portfolio managers are presented with investment ideas from internal buy-side analysts and sell-side analysts from investment banks. It is their job to sift through the relevant information and use their judgment to buy and sell securities. Throughout each day, they read reports, talk to company managers and monitor industry and economic trends looking for the right company and time to invest the portfolio's capital.

A team of analysts and researchers are ultimately responsible for establishing an investment strategy; selecting appropriate investments; and allocating each investment properly for a fund or asset-management vehicle.

Portfolio managers make decisions about investment mix and policy, matching investments to objectives, asset allocation for individuals and institutions, and balancing risk against performance.

Potential Property - Property that you do not owe at present but can afford.

Precious Metals - Any of the less common and highly valuable metals (i.e. gold, silver and platinum).

Principal Reduction– This is a type of debt restructuring that allows a private or public company -- or a sovereign entity facing cash flow problems and financial distress -- to reduce and renegotiate its delinquent debts in order to improve or restore liquidity so that it can continue its operations.

Profit - A financial gain, especially the difference between the amount earned and the amount spent in buying, operating or producing something.

Promissory Note – Also known as a *bank note*, this is a legal instrument (more particularly, a financial instrument), in which one party (the maker or issuer) promises in writing to pay a determinate sum of money to the other (the payee), either at a fixed or determinable future time or on demand of the payee, under specific terms. If the promissory note is unconditional and readily salable, it is called a negotiable instrument.

Referred to as a note payable in accounting (as distinguished from accounts payable), or commonly as just a "note", it is internationally defined by the Convention providing a uniform law for bills of exchange and promissory notes, although regional variations exist. *Bank note* is frequently referred to as a promissory note: a promissory note made by a bank and payable to bearer on demand. Mortgage notes are another prominent example.

Definition and usage of promissory notes are internationally established by the Convention providing a uniform law for bills of exchange and promissory notes, signed in Geneva in 1930. Article

75 of the treaty stated that a promissory note shall contain:

- the term *promissory note* inserted in the body of the instrument and expressed in the language employed in drawing up the instrument;

- an unconditional promise to pay a determinate sum of money;

- a statement of the time of payment;

- a statement of the place where payment is to be made;

- the name of the person to whom or to whose order payment is to be made;

- a statement of the date and of the place where the promissory note is issued;

- the signature of the person who issues the instrument (maker).

In the United States, a promissory note that meets certain conditions is a negotiable instrument regulated by Article 3 of the Uniform Commercial Code. Negotiable promissory notes called mortgage notes are used extensively in combination with mortgages in the financing of real estate transactions.

One prominent example is the Fannie Mae model standard form contract Multistate Fixed-Rate Note 3200, which is publicly available. Promissory notes, or commercial papers, are also issued to provide capital to businesses. However, Promissory Notes act as a source of Finance to the company's creditors.

Promissory notes differ from IOUs in that they contain a specific promise to pay along with the steps and timeline for repayment as well as consequences if repayment fails. IOUs only acknowledging that a debt exists. In common speech, other terms, such as *loan*, *loan agreement*, and *loan contract* may be used interchangeably with *promissory note*, but these terms do not have the same legal meaning. A promissory note is very similar to a loan -- each is a legally binding contract to unconditionally repay a specified amount within a defined time frame -- but a promissory note is generally less detailed and rigid than a loan contract.

For one thing, loan agreements often require repayment in installments, while promissory notes typically do not. Furthermore, a loan agreement usually includes the terms for recourse in the case of default, such as establishing the right to foreclose, while a promissory note does not. Also, while a loan agreement requires signatures from both the borrower and the lender, a promissory note only requires the signature of the borrower.

Negotiable instruments are unconditional and impose few to no duties on the issuer or payee other than payment. In the United States, whether a promissory note is a negotiable instrument can have significant legal impacts, as only negotiable instruments are subject to Article 3 of the Uniform

Commercial Code and the application of the holder in due course rule. The negotiability of mortgage notes has been debated, particularly due to the obligations and "baggage" associated with mortgages; however, mortgages notes are often determined to be negotiable instruments. In the United States, the Non-Negotiable Long Form Promissory Note is not required.

Property - A piece of real estate.

Property Assessment - Property assessment is a process in which a piece of real estate is inspected to determine its real value in contrast to market value.

Property's Equity - The market value of a homeowner's unencumbered interest in their real property. It is the difference between the property's fair market value and the outstanding balance of all liens on the property. The property's equity increases as the debtor makes payments against the mortgage balance, and/or as the property value appreciates.

Property Flippers - Flipping is a term used primarily in the United States to describe purchasing a revenue-generating asset and quickly reselling (or "flipping") it for profit.

Purchase Offer - In business, an offer is a proposal to sell or buy a specific product or service under specific conditions. In the specific case of company stocks, a tender offer is an offer to buy it from existing stockholders under specific conditions.

Offer price, or ask price, is the price a seller is willing to accept for a particular good.

As may be the case with other contracts, real estate contracts may be formed by one party making an offer and another party accepting the offer. To be enforceable, the offers and acceptances must be in writing (Statute of Frauds, Common Law)and signed by the parties agreeing to the contract. Often, the party making the offer prepares a written real estate contract, signs it, and transmits it to the other party who would accept the offer by signing the contract.

As with all other types of legal offers, the other party may accept the offer; reject it (in which case the offer is terminated); make a counteroffer (in which case the original offer is terminated); or not respond to the offer (in which case the offer terminates by the expiration date in it). Before the offer (or counteroffer) is accepted, the offering (or countering) party can withdraw it. A counteroffer may be countered with yet another offer, and a counter-offering process may go on indefinitely between the parties.

To be enforceable, a real estate contract must possess original signatures by the parties and any alterations to the contract must be initialed by all the parties involved. If the original offer is marked up and initialed by the party receiving it, then signed, this is not an offer and acceptance but, rather, a counter-offer.

Rare (Earth) Materials - Rare earth metals is one of a set of seventeen chemical elements in the periodic table, specifically the fifteen lanthanides, as well as scandium and yttrium.

Real Estate - Real estate is property consisting of land and the buildings on it, along with its natural resources such as crops, minerals, or water; immovable property of this nature; an interest vested in this (also) an item of real property; (more generally) buildings or housing in general. Also: the business of real estate; the profession of buying, selling, or renting land, buildings or housing. Major category of real estate property in the U.S. include:

- Attached / multi-unit dwellings
- Apartment – An individual unit in a multi-unit building. The boundaries of the apartment are generally defined by a perimeter of locked or lockable doors. Often seen in multi-story apartment buildings.

- Multi-family house – Often seen in multi-story detached buildings, where each floor is a separate apartment or unit.

- Terraced house (a. k. a. townhouse or rowhouse) – A number of single or multi-unit buildings in a continuous row with shared walls and no intervening space.

- Condominium – Building or complex, similar to apartments, owned by individuals. Common grounds and common areas within the complex are owned and shared jointly. There are townhouse or rowhouse style condominiums as well.

- Cooperative (a. k. a. co-op) – A type of multiple ownership in which the residents of a multi-unit housing complex own shares in the cooperative corporation that owns the property, giving each resident the right to occupy a specific apartment or unit.

- Semi-detached dwellings (in UK, a "semi" is by definition two units with a party wall).

- Duplex – Two units with one shared wall. (in UK, a duplex is an apartment on more than one storey)

- Single-family detached home

- Portable dwellings

- Mobile homes – Potentially a full-time residence which can be (might not in practice be) movable on wheels.

- Houseboats – A floating home

- Tents – Usually very temporary, with roof and walls consisting only of fabric-like material.

Real Estate Agent - A person who sells and rents out buildings and land for clients.

Real Estate Comparison Shopping - This refers to the process of comparing real estate property through appraisals (usually market value).

Real estate transactions require appraisals because they occur infrequently and every property is unique (especially their location, a key factor in valuation), unlike corporate stocks, which are traded daily and are identical (thus a centralized Walrasian auction like a stock exchange is unrealistic). Appraiser reports form the basis for mortgage loans, settling estates and divorces, taxation, and so on. Sometimes the report is used by both parties to set the sale price of a property.

Most, but not all, countries require appraisers to be licensed or certified. Appraisers are often known as *property valuers* or *land valuers*. If the appraiser's opinion is based on market value, then it must also be based on the highest and best use of the real property. For mortgage valuations of improved U.S. residential properties, appraisals are generally reported on a standardized form like the Uniform Residential Appraisal Report. Appraisals of more complex properties (e.g., income-producing, raw land) usually include a narrative appraisal report.

Real Estate Insurance - Real insurance premium is usually part of the real estate mortgage payment. The insurance premium protects lenders against losses that can occur when borrower defaults on the mortgage loan. Mortgage insurance is required for borrowers who make a down payment of less than 20% of the purchase price.

Real Estate Portfolio - A collection of real estate properties held by an investor. Portfolios may be held by individual investors and/or managed by financial professionals, hedge funds, banks and other financial institutions. It is a generally accepted principle that a portfolio is designed according to the investor's risk tolerance, time frame and investment objectives.

Real Estate Pundits- Someone who is an expert in real estate.

Reasonable Price - A price that is fair for both the parties involved.

Recession - A period of temporary economic decline during which trade and industrial activity are reduced, generally identified by a fall in GDP in two successive quarters. A recession is a business cycle contraction. It is a general slowdown in economic activity.

Macroeconomic indicators -- such as GDP , investment spending, capacity utilization, household income, business profits and inflation -- fall, while bankruptcies and the unemployment rate rise. Recessions generally occur when there is a widespread drop in spending (an adverse demand shock). This may be triggered by various events, including a financial crisis, an external trade shock, an adverse supply shock or the bursting of an economic bubble. Governments usually respond to recessions by adopting expansionary macroeconomic policies, such as increasing money supply, increasing government spending and decreasing taxation.

A recession has many attributes that can occur simultaneously and include declines in component measures of economic activity (GDP) such as consumption, investment, government spending, and net export activity. These summary measures reflect underlying drivers such as employment levels and skills, household savings rates, corporate investment decisions, interest rates, demographics, and government policies.

Refinancing - Replacement of old debt by new debt -- when not under financial distress -- is called refinancing.

Renovations – Actions taken to restore something to a better/good condition; make new or as if new again; repair.

REO Property - Real-Estate Owned (REO) is a term used in the United States to describe a class of property owned by a lender -- typically a bank, government agency, or government loan insurer -- after an unsuccessful sale at a foreclosure auction.

Repayment Schedule - A table detailing each periodic payment on a loan. Repayment refers to the process of paying off a debt (often from a loan or mortgage) over time through regular payments.

Resell (Property) - Buying new and used products cheaply and reselling them for a profit.

Residential Property - Property which is zoned for single-family homes; multi-family apartments; townhouses; condominiums; and/or co-ops.

Returns - The gain or loss of a security in a particular period. The return consists of the income and the capital gains relative on an investment. It is usually quoted as a percentage.

Risk - Exposure (someone or something valued) to danger, harm, or loss.

Risks can come from different ways and forms (e.g. uncertainty in financial markets, threats from project failures -- at any phase in design, development, production, or sustainment life-cycles -- legal liabilities, credit risk, accidents, natural causes and disasters as well as deliberate attack from an adversary, or events of uncertain or unpredictable root-cause).

There are two types of events: negative and positive. Negative events can be classified as risks while positive events are classified as opportunities. Several risk management standards have been developed including the Project Management Institute; the National Institute of Standards and Technology; actuarial societies; and ISO standards. Methods, definitions and goals vary widely according to whether the risk management method is in the context of project management; security; engineering; industrial processes; financial portfolios; actuarial assessments; or public health and safety.

For the most part, these methods consist of the following elements, performed, more or less, in the following order.

1. Identify, characterize threats;

2. Assess the vulnerability of critical assets to specific threats;

3. Determine the risk (i.e. the expected likelihood and consequences of specific types of attacks on specific assets);

4. Identify ways to reduce those risks; and

5. Prioritize risk reduction measures based on a strategy.

Sales Letter - A piece of direct mail that is designed to persuade the reader to purchase a particular product or service in the absence of a salesman. It is essentially a type of direct-to-audience mail in which an advertiser sends a letter to a potential customer. It is distinct from other direct mail techniques, such as the distribution of leaflets and catalogues, as the sales letter typically sells a single product or product line, and further tends to be mainly textual as opposed to graphics-based. It is typically used for products or services which, due to their price, are a considered purchase at medium or high value (typically tens to thousands of dollars). A sales letter is often, but not exclusively, the last stage of the sales process before the customer places an order, and is designed to ensure that the prospect is committed to becoming a customer.

Secured Loan - An amount of money lent out in which the borrower pledges some asset (e.g. a car or property) as collateral for the loan, which then becomes a secured debt.

Security Interest - A security interest is a property interest created by agreement or by operation of law over assets to secure the performance of an obligation, usually the payment of a debt.

Seller-Financed Notes - Seller financed notes are a loan that is provided by the seller of a property where no money has been loaned to the buyer. Also called vendor/owner finance or owner carry back, this is a good way for both the owner of the property to sell and also for a buyer to get into the property market or secure property if they found it difficult to secure a loan amount.

Servicing the Note - The process by which a financial company collects interest, principal and escrow payments from a borrower.

Shares - Shares represent a fraction of ownership in a business.

A business may declare different types (classes) of shares, each having distinctive ownership rules, privileges, or share values. Ownership of shares may be documented by issuance of a stock certificate. A stock certificate is a legal document that specifies the amount of shares owned by the shareholder, and other specifics of the shares, such as the par value, if any, or the class of the shares.

Shooting Prices - High prices; prices that have increased significantly in a short amount of time.

Short Refinance Program - A transaction in which the lender agrees to refinance the borrower's home for the current market value, in effect making it more cost effective for the borrower. In it, the lender agrees to replace the lenders current loan with a new one and pays off the difference. This new loan typically has a lower balance, and borrowers typically receive a new interest rate, which is often lower than their former one -- resulting in a reduced mortgage payment.

A short refinance takes place when the borrower's loan balance is more than the property's worth. This is often attributable to declining markets, such as in the recession of 2009, which stressed the financial system's ability to supply mortgage credit, subsequently limiting the ability of Americans to refinance mortgages and buy homes.

Short refinancing is beneficial for both the lender and the borrower, as it enables the borrower to avoid foreclosure and allows them to keep their home, while the bank takes a smaller loss than they would have otherwise with a foreclosure.

Federal Housing Administration short refinance options make it easier for a borrower to short refinance their home. These new guidelines were developed to help borrowers with negative equity. The new guidelines were developed to help borrowers who defaulted on their loans through no fault of their own. The new modifications give more flexibility to *mortgage servicers* (the person you contact if you have questions about your mortgage loan account)as well as to the originators to help unemployed homeowners.

These changes are being funded with $50 billion allocated to housing programs by the Troubled Asset

Relief Program. These programs were developed to help responsible homeowners, such as those who continually made their payments on time, to avoid foreclosure. The current mortgage servicers of borrowers' home loans are under no government requirements to entertain a short payoff refinance which is why most borrowers find it is beneficial to hire a mortgage broker that employs specialized negotiators to take care of the short negotiating for the borrowers (mortgagors). Once an agreement has been reached, a new FHA lender will be required to refinance the loan.

Short Sale - A sale of real estate in which the proceeds from selling the property will fall short of the balance of debts secured by liens against the property. Short sale agreements do not necessarily release borrowers from their obligations to repay any shortfalls on the loans, unless specifically agreed to between the parties. However in certain states, such as California, once the short sale is approved, no deficiencies are permitted after the short sale. (SB 931, SB 458 - Calif. Code of Civil Procedure §580e).

Social Security Number - In the United States, a Social Security number (SSN) is a nine-digit number issued to U.S. citizens, permanent residents, and temporary (working) residents under Section 205(c)(2) of the Social Security Act, codified as 42 U.S.C. § 405(c)(2). The number is issued to an individual by the Social Security Administration, an independent agency of the United States government. Although its primary purpose is to track individuals for Social Security purposes, the Social Security number has become a de facto national identification number for taxation and other purposes. A Social Security number may be obtained by applying on Form SS-5, "Application for A Social Security Number Card."

The Internal Revenue Service (IRS) offers alternatives to SSNs in some places where providing untrusted parties with identification numbers is essential. Tax return preparers must obtain and use a

Preparer Tax Identification Number (PTIN) to include on their client's tax returns (as part of signature requirements). Day care services have tax benefits, and even a sole proprietor should give parents an EIN (employer identification number) to use on their tax return.

The Social Security Administration has suggested that, if asked to provide his or her Social Security number, a citizen should ask which law requires its use. In accordance with §7213 of the 9/11 Commission Implementation Act of 2004 and 20 C.F.R. 422.103(e)(2), the number of replacement Social Security cards per person is generally limited to three per calendar year and ten in a lifetime.

Spreadsheet - A spreadsheet is an interactive computer application program for organization, analysis and storage of data in tabular form.

Starting Cost – The expenses incurred when setting up and beginning a business. This business start-up cost includes legal fees; office supplies and equipment; and marketing costs, as well as the expenses that will keep you running, (i.e. payroll, monthly expenses, inventory).

Stock - A share of a company that entitles the holder to a fixed dividend, whose payment takes priority over that of common-stock dividends.

The stock (also known as *capital stock*) of a corporation constitutes the equity stake of its owners. It represents the residual assets of the company that would be due to stockholders after discharge of all senior claims such as secured and unsecured debt. Stockholders' equity cannot be withdrawn from the company in a way that is intended to be detrimental to the company's creditors. The stock of a corporation is partitioned into shares, the total of which are stated at the time of business formation. Additional shares subsequently may be authorized by the existing shareholders and issued by the company. In some jurisdictions, each share of stock has a certain declared par value, which is a nominal accounting value used to represent the equity on the balance sheet of the corporation. In other jurisdictions, however, shares of stock may be issued without associated par value.

Stock Exchange - A stock exchange is a place or organization by which stock traders (people and companies) can trade stocks. Companies may want to get their stock listed on a stock exchange. Other stocks may be traded *over the counter*, that is, through a dealer. A large company will usually have its stock listed on many exchanges across the world. Exchanges may also cover other types of security such as fixed interest securities or indeed derivatives.

Stock Market - The market in which shares of publicly held companies are issued and traded either through exchanges or over-the-counter markets.

A stock market or equity market is the aggregation of buyers and sellers (a loose network of economic transactions, not a physical facility or discrete entity) of stocks (also called shares); these may include securities listed on a stock exchange as well as those only traded privately.

Stocks can be categorized in various ways. One common way is, by the country where the company is domiciled. For example, Nestlé and Novartis are domiciled in Switzerland, so they may be considered as part of the Swiss stock market, although their stock may also be traded at exchanges in other countries.

Market participants include individual retail investors, institutional investors such as mutual funds, banks, insurance companies and hedge funds, and also publicly traded corporations trading in their own shares. Some studies have suggested that institutional investors and corporations trading in their own shares generally receive higher risk-adjusted returns than retail investors.

A few decades ago, worldwide, buyers and sellers were individual investors, such as wealthy businessmen, usually with long family histories to particular corporations. Over time, markets have become more "institutionalized"; buyers and sellers are largely institutions (e.g., pension funds, insurance companies, mutual funds, index funds, exchange-traded funds, hedge funds, investor groups, banks and various other financial institutions).

The rise of the institutional investor has brought with it some improvements in market operations. There has been a gradual tendency for "fixed" (and exorbitant) fees being reduced for all investors, partly from falling administration costs but also assisted by large institutions challenging brokers' oligopolistic approach to setting standardized fees.

Spur the Price - Increase the price.

Stream of Cash - Source of income.

Strict Foreclosure - This type of foreclosure, which is available in a few states including Connecticut, New Hampshire and Vermont, brings suit by the mortgagee. If successful, a court orders the defaulted mortgagor to pay the mortgage within a specified period of time. Should the mortgagor fail to do so, the mortgage holder gains the title to the property with no obligation to sell it. This type of foreclosure is generally available only when the value of the property is less than the debt (also said to be *under water*). Historically, strict foreclosure was the original method of foreclosure. Because of its limited availability to only a few states, this type of foreclosure is considered minor, bearing in mind that it still is a foreclosure.

The process of foreclosure can be rapid or lengthy and varies from state to state. Other options such as refinancing, a short sale, alternate financing, temporary arrangements with the lender, or even bankruptcy, may present homeowners with ways to avoid it altogether. Websites which can connect individual borrowers and homeowners to lenders are increasingly offered as mechanisms to bypass traditional lenders while meeting payment obligations for mortgage providers. Although there are slight differences between the states, the foreclosure process generally follows a timeline beginning with initial missed payments, moving to a sale being scheduled and finally a redemption period (if available).

Subordinate Lien - Also known as a *second-lien mortgage* or *junior-lien mortgage*; When this exists, and the borrower goes into foreclosure, the lender of this mortgage will be paid only after the first-lien mortgage is paid off. A subordinate-lien mortgage is generally "higher-priced" if the APR of this mortgage is 3.5 percentage points or more higher than the APOR.

Target Market – A target market is a group of customers towards which a business has decided to aim its marketing efforts and ultimately its merchandise. A well-defined target market is the first element of a successful real estate strategy. Target markets are groups of individuals that are separated by distinguishable and noticeable aspects.

Target markets can be separated by segmentations such as:

- addresses (their location, climate, region);

- demographic/socioeconomic segmentation (gender, age, income, occupation, education, household size and stage in the family life cycle);

- psychographic segmentation (similar attitudes, values, and lifestyles),

- behavioral segmentation (occasions, degree of loyalty); and

- product-related segmentation - (relationship to a product).

Tenant - A person who occupies land or property rented from a landlord.

Title of House's Ownership - A title is a bundle of rights in a piece of property in which a party may own either a legal interest or equitable interest.

Title Record Search - In real estate business and law, this is the process of retrieving documents evidencing events in the history of a piece of real estate property in order to determine relevant interests in and regulations concerning that property. It is also known as a *title search* or *property title search*.

A title search is performed when an owner wishes to mortgage his property, and the bank requires the owner to insure this transaction. Anyone may do a title search. Documents concerning conveyances of land are a matter of public record. These documents are maintained in hard copy paper format or sometimes scanned into image files. The information within the documents is typically not available as data format as the records are descriptions of legal events which contain terms, conditions, and language in excess of data.

Trend - A general direction in which something is developing or changing.

A market trend is a tendency of financial markets to move in a particular direction over time [see *market trend*]. These trends are classified as secular for long time frames; primary for medium time frames; and secondary for short time frames. Traders identify market trends using technical analysis, a framework which characterizes market trends as predictable price tendencies within the market when price reaches support and resistance levels, varying over time.

Strictly, a trend can only be determined in hindsight, since at any time prices in the future are not known.

This does not prevent people from prognosticating about future trends.

The terms *bull market* and *bear market* describe upward and downward market trends, respectively, and can be used to describe either the market as a whole or specific sectors and securities.

Undeveloped Land - Land that has not yet been built upon. This land tends to be reserved/used for uses like houses, businesses and industrial facilities.

Vacant Property - (Of premises) Having no fixtures, furniture, or inhabitants; empty.

Valuable Minerals - Valuable minerals are minerals that have considerable financial worth.

Virtual Business - A virtual business employs electronic or other means to transact business as opposed to a traditional brick and mortar business that relies on face-to-face transactions with physical documents and physical currency or credit.

Water Lien - Water/sewer is a lienable utility and will stay on the title of a property until it is paid in full, either by means of a check, a refinance or a sale.

Win-Win Situation - A situation where both the parties gain.

Workout – An out-of-court restructuring as it pertains to refinancing. This is increasingly becoming a global reality.

Write-Off (Inventory) - A reduction of the recognized value of something. In accounting, this is a recognition of the reduced or zero value of an asset. In income tax statements, this is a reduction of taxable income, as a recognition of certain expenses required to produce the income.

Yellow Pages™ - A telephone directory of businesses, organized by category (rather than alphabetically by business name) and in which advertising is sold. The directories were originally printed on yellow paper, as opposed to white pages for non-commercial listings. The traditional term Yellow Pages™ now also applied to online directories of businesses.

Sources:

http://www.investopedia.com

http://www.businessdictionary.com

http://www.businessdictionaries.org

http://dictionary.reference.com/browse/BUSINESS

http://www.oxforddictionaries.com/definition/english/business

Acknowledgments

We are known in the industry as the Kings of Debt but we didn't become Kings all on our own. We would like to recognize, acknowledge and applaud all the people around the world that helped us make it. We cannot name you all by name, but you know who you are. We salute you and we are honored to serve with you on this noble mission of educating the world about the mortgage note business.

We would like to specifically highlight and mention those individuals who were directly instrumental in the writing and publishing of this book and our lives:

Our mothers are number one. We both refer to our mothers as our *mama dukes*. Without them we wouldn't be here or anywhere. For their love and courage, we thank them.

One of us is lucky to have the greatest father known to men. Thanks to him, we are both very blessed.
Ευχαριστώ πατέρας μου..

Ildi: You have always been an angelic blessing.

Little Dimitri: For being the light and joy of your uncle's life...

Tasha and Ted for just not making little Dimitri, but for also being an amazing sister and an amazing brother in law.

Nick Tang for always believing in our capabilities and extending his amazing talents and know-how with his national conferences.

Stacks "Street Legend" for holding it down and keeping it real from the beginning, repping Queens to the fullest.

Jack Krupey for always being a good friend and a wealth of information that we can count on.

Luw Sookpaul of CNS and Associates for his expertise and no-stone-unturned attitude when it comes to taxes.

Alex Goldovsky for always giving us the time and support when due diligence was crucial.

Cristal y Yazmin por ser las mejores amigas.

The Conde's for awakening the art collectors in us.

A big shout out to the original and one and only WIN (Women In Notes): Cathie Jeffs and Cathy Cray, also known as the Queens of Debt. They are amazing and true professionals in the note business.

Jag Sookpaul of Business Technology Services for his amazing IT support that from the beginning has proven to be invaluable.

A special thanks to the very beautiful Maria Bello for being the editor of this book.

We would also like to thank the naysayers and the ones that couldn't wait for our success proving that you didn't possess the winning demeanor and strength to stick by, leaving us early. As much as that hurt us, we thank you.

ADDITIONAL COURSES ON DEBT INVESTMENTS BY THE AUTHORS

The below subjects and materials by Dean Anastos and Ricky Brava are meticulously designed to prepare you for success in the note and debt business. They include:

Detailed Documentation on the Industry

Real Case Studies on Real Files

Bank Asset Liquidation

Mortgage Note Exchange

Hard Money Lending

Fund Investing

Collaborative Note Investing

Private Placement Memorandum Advisory

Examinations for you to grade your progress

About the Authors

Dean Anastos was raised in Queens, New York by Greek and Cuban immigrant parents. He learned about the real estate industry early on from his father. Dean has been an entrepreneur as far back as he remembers. He made his wealth when he founded Resilicon in 2001, generating over $7 million in his first year of operation by buying up used Cisco equipment from dot-com companies that went bust and reselling that equipment through Internet channels. He then invested the proceeds into real estate, amassing over 120 rental properties. When the real estate crash happened in 2008, Dean lost a substantial portion of his wealth; however, in that process he learned about the debt game from the bank's perspective. Dean founded Apollo Financial Group and brought on the very talented Ricky Brava as a partner. Dean is now bringing this very lucrative and secret style of investing to the masses.

Ricky Brava has always had a natural ability for sales and business. Raised in Queens, New York, his entrepreneurial spirit took flight at a young age when, as a child, he collected soda cans from the neighborhood with other childhood friends and turning them in for change, eventually making enough money to buy comic books that he later sold for profit. Always creating profitable scenarios for everyone he comes in touch with, Ricky has had the pleasure of giving a speech for the Greater Los Angeles MENSA society on the subject of mentoring. He currently appears at speaking engagements nationwide. From humble beginnings to the top of the note business, he is proud of his journey and promises to share it in later books.

NOTES (no pun intended)

www.mortgagefloat.com

www.apollofinancialgrp.com

www.ingramcontent.com/pod-product-compliance
Lightning Source LLC
Chambersburg PA
CBHW070338240426
43665CB00045B/2189